I0464317

CARIBBEAN: ECONOMICS, MIGRANTS AND CONTROL

CARIBBEAN: ECONOMICS, MIGRANTS AND CONTROL

An analysis of Socio-Cultural and Economic Dependence

GLADSTONE F. GREENE, Ph.D

Copyright © 2013 by Gladstone F. Greene, Ph. D

Library of Congress Control Number:		2013904026
ISBN:	Hardcover	978-1-4836-0453-4
	Softcover	978-1-4836-0452-7
	Ebook	978-1-4836-0454-1

All rights reserved. No part of this book may be reproduced or transmitted
in any form or by any means, electronic or mechanical, including photocopying,
recording, or by any information storage and retrieval system,
without permission in writing from the copyright owner.

This book was printed in the United States of America.

Rev. date: 08/03/2013

To order additional copies of this book, contact:
Xlibris Corporation
1-888-795-4274
www.Xlibris.com
Orders@Xlibris.com
130504

CONTENTS

Chapter 1: Overview of Present Sociohistorical and Demographic Status 7

Chapter 2: The Extent of Sociocultural Control 22

Chapter 3: Returning Resources and Remittances 33

Chapter 4: Migration and Control 41

Chapter 5: The Global Economic Issues and the Caribbean 48

Some concluding observations 53

Appendix 55

Bibliography 81

Index 83

CHAPTER 1

Overview of Present Sociohistorical and Demographic Status

After political independence was achieved, many Caribbean countries, if not all, expected that this achievement would spread throughout other areas of national development significance. One of these areas was, of course, economic, and the other was sociocultural. However, many nations would soon find out and become disappointed when the advances in these areas were nonexistent or pedestrian at best. What was seen as a period of rising expectations became a period of complaints, accusations, and in some cases, a wish to return to the previous situation. This was in relatively "stable" times. Countries still had their economic navel strings tied to the mother countries insomuch that the political independence won seemed to be of no consequence.

States continued to look to and depend on the "outside" whenever problems were experienced, such as appointing foreign administrators to head vital sectors, including the police force, to manage and solve their crime issues or to investigate fraud and other crimes that developed. Some states had their justice system still tied to the former colonial country. Others invited the former colonizers to remain and help set up their new postindependence institutions.

The reverse side was that the former colonial masters imposed very harsh conditions for their help with regard to the IMF and World Bank. Soon industries that flourished in the preindependence period contracted while others collapsed altogether and new ones were difficult to establish. In addition, the resentment and bitterness emanating from the independence struggle led multinational companies to impose high prices for raw materials, machineries, spare parts, and skills that were necessary to create or stimulate growth and consolidation in the newly independent nations. It was soon realized that political independence was not an end but a very painful beginning.

The independent Caribbean countries' total continued dependence on pre-1960s economy of sugar, rice (Guyana), bananas, and bauxite (Guyana and Jamaica) went under serious stress. Coupled with problems of maintaining viability of the industries and paying for equipment and spare parts with foreign exchange was the unintended backlash on the labor force, the inability to pay wages and improve working conditions, etc. In the labor-intensive industries, which provided the bulk of the politicians' support, workers reasonably expected an improved slice of the pie than what existed in the previous system while meeting the IMF's sometimes-impossible conditions.

Some scholars and political observers, both local and foreign, blamed nationalization in Guyana: Burnham's policy of taking control of the "commanding heights of the economy" for that nation's problems. The critics seemed to have been correct when sugar couldn't sustain itself, made worse by constant industrial conflicts and the lack of spare parts for the factories. Many sugar factories had to be closed or combined with others to maintain some sort of production efficiency and viability. The result was that total sugar and rice production dropped, and this affected many sectors of the economy. These products were claimed to be the "mainstay of the country's economy." The failure of some major development projects highly involved the *Brazil road project*, the financial suspicions surrounding multilateral schools' projects (University of Guyana lecture buildings), the investments in road transportation after the railway was abolished, the glass factory, the ham-and-bacon factory project, the hydropower project—which came to a very angry, abrupt, and unfortunate demise—prompted Burnham to promise "building the country with our fingernails."

All these were part of a long list of development disasters for Guyana. Other Caribbean countries did not fare much better, and their infrastructure continued to spiral downward. In fact, Caribbean political independence ushered in greater dependence on foreign support in order to subsist, sometimes from the very colonial countries or their multinational surrogates.

Scholars were warning about these eventual developments very soon after the independence events of the major Caribbean countries—George Beckford's

Persistent Poverty: Underdevelopment in Plantation (1972) and *Caribbean Economy: Dependency and Backwardness* (1975) and Martin Ravallion's *Growth Inequality and Poverty* (2001), to name a few.

The major factors consistent in these writings are (a) the decline of world sugar prices, (b) the increased competition from beet sugar, (c) the general decline of agricultural productivity, and (d) the failure of Caribbean countries to develop secondary industries, thereby cushioning the impact of the decline of the major preindependence economy.

This failure of growth of the economies of several Caribbean countries after political independence was also the concern of Lloyd Best in his early analysis "Character of the Caribbean Economy," a paper on the state-biased growth through the exploitation of surplus labor. Best, like other Caribbean economists referred to earlier, saw and recognized the need for a dynamic manufacturing sector as a source of sustainable growth and employment. The latter, Best later suggests, would open markets for products not only around the region but internationally as well. The struggle of the Caribbean countries for economic independence continued into the 1980s and 1990s with very few signs of economic prosperity.

Then came the global economic crisis, and it exposed the vulnerability of some of these countries to further economic pain and disaster.

Several areas of national development were impacted by what followed. These included (a) the reduction of volume of exports and GDP, (b) the redistribution of the terms of trade, (c) the reduction of tourism receipts including remittances, (d) the difficulty of acquiring foreign financing and coping with the additional conditions therein, and (e) the collapse of investments and insurance protection. According to *Rodrik* (2009), "Slower world trade growth, less abundant foreign financing, contraction of the more regulated financial system, less appetite for risk on the part of investors, bankers, businesses and savers filtered across the Caribbean sea causing consternation to more vulnerable, less organized economies."

Despite unsustainable public debt for Guyana (78% external and 37% domestic), Jamaica (51% external and 66.9% domestic), and Trinidad and Tobago (6.4% external and 12.6% domestic), many other countries tried unsuccessfully to cope by limiting fiscal space due to deficits and excessive debt stocks. However, some managed to introduce countercyclicality through a combination of larger public investment and higher social spending. Others like Grenada, Barbados, and Antigua are being forced to pay more attention to domestic markets to enhance growth and productive diversification.

Many scholars have pointed to the small size of individual markets, which make the latter almost impossible, creating another look at redoubling efforts toward regional integration, both within and without CARICOM. The point being made is for these small economies to increase value-added financing in tourism and other sectors by generating more sophisticated products and diversifying the supply of services.

Ronald Saunders (2012) argues that "the importance of the Caribbean Community (CARICOM) acting jointly to address their development needs has become acute." Saunders contends that given the high levels of debt to GDP ratios, the widening budget deficits, the deteriorating terms of trade, the dwindling aid flows and shocks to their economies due to a decline of tourism earnings, and the grave concern of the financial services sector, the majority of CARICOM countries are reeling.

Saunders asserts that Caribbean countries "must be prepared to show how aid will be used effectively to diversifying their economies, enhancing their productive sector, and standing on their own two [collective] feet." But with the strict conditions being imposed on countries that seek aid, this move will be impossible to effect.

Trade specialist *David Lewis* expressed misgivings that the Caribbean governments will act in a meaningful way. This is so simply because they are so out of touch with reality in politics and economics, trying to play catch-up. Lewis is supported by several EU representatives in the Caribbean who lamented that Caribbean governments have not actively pursued funding for regional projects that would benefit their countries individually as well as the region collectively. Other commentators have been blunter, arguing that in their "beggar-thy neighbor and nonproductive approach," many CARICOM governments have sought solutions to their economic problems in essentially national efforts, shunning the real benefits that could derive from regional action as well.

According to the Global Review Index of Caribbean Economic Freedoms (2008-2011), of the countries under consideration, none of the countries fared very well while trying to cope in any fiscal area, with fiscal and political corruption being the major stumbling blocks.

In order to cope with the impact of the global crises, small developing countries like those in the Caribbean would need to implement a new set of *macroeconomic policies* and *practices* on two major fronts:

A. *Fiscal policy*: Secure and keep foreign lending on terms that would allow them to switch the existing composition of public debt toward "lower interests and longer maturities." This system, it is argued, would create fiscal space to the point of establishing debt-to-GDP constancy while creating and operating effective sectorial polices.

B. *Monetary policy*: One of the many criticisms of the economies of the major West Indian countries—Jamaica, Trinidad and Tobago, Barbados (to a lesser extent), and certainly Guyana—is their inability to monitor, control, and even reduce domestic inflation. The aim, of course, is to prevent the countries' real exchange rate from appreciating.

Linked with these policies is the provision of preferential credit to local priority activities through public financial institutions. In the past, these attempts have resulted in massive public corruption and fraud with many of the projects left incomplete and the government officials being blamed for poor financial control or being part of the criminal activities themselves.

Much has been written and exposed about the massive corruption that continues to plague Guyana, Trinidad, Jamaica, and some of the smaller states. Multimillion-dollar contracts for development projects were said to be awarded to companies on the basis of "kickbacks" to politicians. Many such companies were overseas based and did not appear to go through the normal process required of tenders or have the particular interests of these nations foremost. One source listed the following as some examples: NICIL, lotto funds, Chinese contractors undertaking major projects in both Guyana and Trinidad, GP & Light cable scandal, one-laptop-per-family scandal, airport projects in both Trinidad and Guyana, and ongoing corruption scandals in Jamaica.

Another analyst has contended that "something has gone horribly wrong in postindependent Jamaica and the country which orchestrated the break-up of the West Indies Federation has not been better off since its independence" (Ian Thompson, *The Dead Yard*).

Overall, Jamaica did not fare well, at least socioeconomically, as inequalities on all fronts remain very strong. Jamaica continues to have high poverty and unemployment rates. Even though its tourism, bauxite, and some agriculture sectors are still profitable, social inequalities persist. People with a more European "look" and Asians seem to have a better lien on economics and other positions than people from the local black majority. In addition, poverty, violence and crime (gang and gun activities), unemployment, and the advent of "dons" have all become increasing liabilities on the struggling Jamaican society.

Lack of financial controls and making financial support contingent on the achievement of performance goals should be strictly adhered to.

Many of these Caribbean countries have been reluctant, at best, to even consider the underlying conditions, especially their impact on the domestic economy. But such risk taking, scholars argue, might be necessary to be shielded from future downturns. On the contrary, it is hard to conceive that these changes could be effective with continued insularity and without the union of economies among these small states. States continue to rely on decisions that are subjugating them to the same harsh conditions that got them in this position in the first place. It is still generally believed by leading commentators that integration is more than necessary to secure and expand the demand for locally produced goods and services and to capture the resources available regionally.

Michael Roberts in "Cultural Imperialism and Integration in the Caribbean, Part III" writes that "there needs to be a rethinking—a revolution in thought—by the region's present leadership in a way that evaluates what the region has, where it is going, what are the existing internal and external threats to regional development and come up with a comprehensive blue-print for the future."

Integration will achieve "critical mass," making it easier to command world respect, economic and political significance, and bargaining clout. The question is, can the Caribbean nations achieve togetherness beyond CARICOM that would allow them to impact the world; negotiate regional, financial, and economic understanding with the multinationals; and stand up to imperialism and neocolonial strategies without giving up their individual nations' independence and identity? So far, what exists as CARICOM grouping does not seem to fit the bill.

All these ideas and questions have been raised before by leading political and other scholars and have confronted the islands political leadership for years. It appears, however, that there is a persistence of the old colonial practices of divide and rule. The present crop of leadership seems not in a position or lacks the courage to recreate the spirit that propelled these islands to political independence and that the postindependence pioneers held dearly. It is from this background that sizeable numbers of the Caribbean-born population are migrating to the United States, Canada, and the United Kingdom.

Present Demographics (Caribbean-Born US Residents)

Demographic data on the Caribbean (West Indian) population, unless specifically mentioned, almost always include English- and non-English-speaking countries.

For the purposes of this review, however, the focus will be on the English-speaking countries. In addition, the data considers *Caribbean-born residents*, including *children born in the Caribbean* and who subsequently join their relatives in the United States. However, since children born in the United States of Caribbean-born parents are considered US citizens, they are not represented in the data.

In 2010, approximately 35.1% of Caribbean-born immigrants reported speaking only English and 25.6% reported speaking English "very well." In contrast, 44.2% of Caribbean immigrants were limited English proficient (LEP), meaning that they reported speaking English less than "very well." Within this group, about 10.0% reported that they did not speak English at all, 17.3% reported speaking English "well," and another 17.5% reported speaking English but "not very well."

Caribbean immigrants were less likely to be LEP than other foreign-born populations overall, of which 52.2% reported limited English proficiency in 2010. Interestingly enough, rates of limited English proficiency vary substantially by Caribbean country of origin even within English-speaking countries but more so with nations of different language origin. For example, almost all immigrants from Saint Kitts (99.2%), Grenada (98.9%), Trinidad and Tobago (98.9%), Jamaica (97.9%), Barbados (99.1%), and Guyana (culturally regarded as Caribbean, 96.8%) reported speaking only English or speaking English "very well." In contrast, 69.4% of immigrants from the Dominican Republic, 65.8% of immigrants from Cuba, and 58.7% of immigrants from Haiti were LEP. A mere 14.3% reported.

According to the data extracted from the *US Census* conducted in 2010, the United States was home to over 3.5 million immigrants from the Caribbean, who accounted for 10.1% of the total foreign-born residents. Although this represents a sizeable portion, most of the foreign-born English-speaking residents, over 2 million, came from Jamaica, Trinidad and Tobago, Guyana, and Barbados.

There has been a significant increase of foreign-born immigrants over the last forty years (over 17%), but this increase was due to the vast numbers of persons arriving from Haiti, the Dominican Republic, and Cuba. The population inflows from the English-speaking Caribbean, however, slowed slightly, and their total share of the foreign-born has declined over the ten years when compared to the total Caribbean population as covered by the census.

Compared to other immigrant groups, the foreign-born populations from the English-speaking Caribbean states were less likely to be new arrivals. The apparent gap between the arrival of parents and their children and other members of the family seems to determine the disparity in the various arrival schedules. Other foreign-born groups, the data reveals, tend to arrive in family clusters and are more likely to do so at the same time.

The practice of parents of other foreign groups immigrating and having their loved ones follow later is less prevalent in the non-Caribbean residents than within the groups in the review. Even with married couples, one partner immigrates and remains for some two to five years before being joined by the other and the rest of the family members. Because of this gap, the level of anxiety to join the folks sometimes results in a high level of illegal immigration. In fact, the rate of unauthorized immigrants among Caribbean immigrants was roughly 3.8%, slightly higher than other Caribbean groups. In the meantime, friction sometimes develops in the family relationship, resulting in the breakup of the family unit. The census data suggests a higher rate of such breakups within the Caribbean foreign-born from the English-speaking countries when compared with the other foreign-born groups.

Within the ten years covered by this census, it seems that there was an increasing number of immigrants between *fifteen and twenty years of age*. In fact, there is a 10% increase of migrating Caribbean peoples in this category. The data from the schools in Brooklyn—especially in the Flatbush and East New York, Crown Heights, and to a lesser extent, Downtown Brooklyn—have a higher rate of newly arrived students in their upper classes. The new arrivals of school-age students within this category are in school while others are seeking college admission or some form of nonspecific employment. There is a recurring issue of correct placement of school-age Caribbean students who arrive with their school documentation. The United States educational authorities still have problems in evaluating the British-based grading system in relation to the Caribbean Exams Council (CXC), secondary schools entrance examination (SSEE), Caribbean secondary education certificate (CSEC), Caribbean certificate of secondary level competence (CCSLC), and even the region's universities' transcripts for school, work, and college admissions. The result is that many such students are either wrongly placed (i.e., put in lower grades than they deserve) or placed in special programs well below their competence after they arrive in the United States.

The other category with increase in new arrivals is the 25 to 35 age groups. The Caribbean region has seen significant numbers of its best-educated citizens emigrate. According to one observer, the emigration rate of college educated (forced and induced) is among the highest in the world among foreign-born populations. For example, an estimated 76% of Jamaicans with a college education migrated to the United States: between 45% and 55% for most of the other countries. Around 25.2% of the 25 to 35 age groups (less than one-sixth) of the total Caribbean-born had at least a bachelor's degree or higher. This compares to about 24% of the total foreign-born population.

While this so-called brain drain has been associated with a loss for the native developing countries and a gain for the developed industrial countries, the present approach, however, by some governments is to turn this "drain" to the advantage of the. This is possible by utilizing the additional skills and training of the formidable diaspora and tapping into their potential resources through *remittances* (see chapter 4).

Shortly after arriving in the new country, the migrants tend to look for work first because of the immediate need for sustenance and upkeep. Relatives and friends usually can only be dependent on accommodation, clothes, and food for a limited time.

According to the census, the number of Caribbean English-speaking residents who were likely to participate in the US labor force was slightly higher than the total Caribbean foreign residents but lower than the total foreign-born from all countries. Of the Caribbean-born new arrivals (within 5 years), over 75% between the ages of 15 and 17 were attending school while the newly arrived between 25 and 35 years of age were either attending college or participating in the labor force as part-time or undocumented workers. Much of this data is very difficult to arrive at for obvious reasons, but the estimates are important when the subject of remittances is considered. In fact, whether the new residents are documented or not, the desire to remit resources for their loved ones back home is very strong. They seek ways to provide some form of support once they are employed through other travelers, if not channeled through an "official" accountable source.

The data for specific Caribbean-born residents who were most likely to become employed include *Anguilla (72.8%), Saint Kitts (70.5%), Jamaica (70.9%), and Guyana (65.7%)*. New immigrants from Trinidad, Barbados, Grenada, Saint Lucia, and Antigua tend to delay their full-time employment until they have completed some schooling, mainly because of the support from home or direct relatives. For Guyana and Jamaica, additionally, the setting up of their own businesses (Brooklyn and Queens) seems to take precedence over working for other individuals and over other activities.

The figures for the unemployed show a greater propensity among the total Caribbean-born new arrivals to be without recorded gainful employment when compared to the total foreign-born population. Of the 18 to 30 age group who were not at school but were legal residents, 8.8% reported that they were unemployed against 6.8% of the total foreign-born and 10.2% of the total non-English-speaking Caribbean.

Occupation	Foreign born		Caribbean born	
	Number	Percent	Number	Percent
Employed civilian population 16 years and older	16,083,670	100.0	1,517,655	100.0
Management, professional, and related occupations	4,574,120	28.4	380,015	25.0
Service occupations	3,214,315	20.0	370,750	24.4
Sales and office occupations	3,208,310	19.9	374,050	24.6
Farming, fishing, and forestry occupations	328,620	2.0	5,547	0.4
Construction, extraction, and maintenance occupations	1,677,340	10.4	137,540	9.1
Production, transportation, and material moving occupations	3,080,970	19.2	249,730	16.5

Table 1. Occupational Comparison of the Caribbean-Born and Foreign-Born Populations in the United States

Source: US Census Bureau, Census 2000, Foreign-Born Profiles, STP-159.

Earnings

While the obvious reluctance among the undocumented to disclose accurate earnings data is understandable, especially when two or more jobs are involved, the data is of great significance in analyzing the economic status of migrants and its impact on remittances.

There appears to be some disparity in the earning rates of English-speaking Caribbean-born and those of other Caribbean countries. This disparity is explained by the differences in the nature of employment. It seems that the foreign-born from *Haiti, Guadeloupe, Aruba, and the Dominican Republic* who speak two and more languages tend to work additional jobs as interpreters and translators and therefore increase their earnings. The data shows that most Caribbean-born from the English-speaking Caribbean are fluent in one language; however, they do not readily attract multiple steady jobs. Many, nonetheless, work more than one part-time job as tutors, home attendants, and nurse aides.

The Caribbean-born men with the highest reported earnings were from *the Dutch island of Aruba ($59,000), the Netherlands Antilles ($55,058),* and *Anguilla ($47,083).* The men with the lowest median earnings were from the *Dominican Republic ($44,839), Haiti ($35,835),* and *the Bahamas ($39,844).* It should be noted that the latter two groups were the two groups with relatively low English fluency and educational levels. These figures do not include income from other sources, including part-time jobs. Additionally, groups of Caribbean-born from the Barbados, Trinidad, Guyana, and Jamaica shared the highest levels of spoken English and had a high school degree or other higher level of education upon arrival.

The data on Caribbean-born residents who were most likely to own their own home shows that the population from the English-speaking states was least likely to own homes in the United States or elsewhere. When compared to other Caribbean-born residents (53.8%) and all foreign-born (48.7%), the percentage for the English-speaking Caribbean tends to be lower (34.3%).

Many analysts attribute this to two factors. The first is the overwhelming desire among these working groups to make sacrifices and to send as much resources back home. These resources are mostly used to purchase, build, or repair their homes in their native countries or set up small arcade-type businesses or stalls in the larger markets. They may, therefore, have less resources remaining in their new environment and have to rent or share accommodation temporarily.

The other reason is the transitory or temporary nature of the stay abroad. Many Caribbean migrants, especially from the English-speaking states, emigrate with the ultimate desire of returning to their native countries eventually. They therefore tend to prepare for that day. It is true that some never return, but returning home always remains an option.

The culture of allocation of earnings for temporary livelihood and home ownership are factors that impact negatively on the general quality of life of the Caribbean-born population. In the 10 years that precede the 2010 census, 19.3% of all foreign-born populations were living below the poverty line compared to 12.5% of the general population. Of course, this data assumes a set of income thresholds that vary by family size, composition, and allocation.

The 2010 earnings data show that the median earnings of Caribbean-born men ($32,000) who provide over 15% of the remittances were slightly lower than the foreign-born but higher than the workingmen from the English-speaking Caribbean. The men with the highest earnings ($40,000) seem to be from the Dutch islands of Aruba and the Netherlands Antilles. One reason given for the disparity of earnings among the Caribbean-born is their desire to work more than one job for the first 5 years that they emigrate. After that, the trend suggests that they settle down and focus on one full-time legal job or, at best, two jobs, by which time some permanency is acquired.

In terms of the women from the English-speaking Caribbean, their initial earnings compare favorably with the median earnings from the total foreign-born but are slightly higher than those of other Caribbean-born women ($28,000). These women tend to allocate as much as 25% of their total earnings to remittances in cash, materials, or to pay the travel expenses of their loved ones.

By the year 2010, 49.9% of Caribbean-born residents owned their own homes compared to 21.3% of residents from the English-speaking Caribbean and 43.0% of all foreign-born. This represents an overall increase of approximately 13.6% over the 2000 data. It is believed the many new arrivals from the non-English-speaking Caribbean (Haiti and Dominican Republic) tend to secure households earlier in an effort to accommodate their loved ones who are then encouraged to migrate. However, this practice is observed among all foreign-born to varying degrees.

The Caribbean-born householders who are most likely to own their own homes were from the Cayman Islands (63.3%), Aruba (60.1%), and Cuba

(58.2%). The Caribbean-born householders least likely to own their own homes were from the Dominican Republic (20.0%), Saint Lucia (37.6%), and Guadeloupe (37.7%). In these examples, the new populations tend to settle in or eventually move to areas where similar nationalities live rather than set up new communities. In addition, many of the older settlers tend to provide or be involved in real estate businesses and can easily relate to providing accommodation and employment to the new arrivals.

In postindependence Caribbean, the desire to continue to look abroad for solutions to internal problems appears to have been born out of their colonial experience. While, on the surface, there does not seem to be anything disconcerting about this desire, it appears to be a dependency mind-set. Political independence produced a culture of rising expectations. The migration practice, which originated from the lack of specific existing foundations, is capable of providing education, jobs, and the attractiveness of modern society. Postindependence Caribbean nations had to contend with tremendous "teething problems," many of which became unbearable to their citizens, thereby increasing the desire to migrate. Jamaican folklorist *Ms. Lou*, after observing this phenomenon, was prompted to write that "Jamaica was colonizing England in reverse."

The nations became very vulnerable to exploitation of their human capital resources in a way that led to draining of the very qualified minds that were expected to remain loyal and help in the construction of the new societies. The three major foreign countries that proved the most attractive were *Canada*, *the United States*, and *Britain*. Since the latter was the former colonial power, many found its societal culture and practices to be consistent with their own ambitions. Hence, it was understandable that many English-speaking Caribbean students opted to study to become doctors, lawyers, and engineers and receive other professional training in their former mother country.

What is very significant now is the extent to which there a "new colonial hand" is reaching out to replace this old power. Caribbean citizens are being exposed aggressively to situations to prepare their *minds* and *behaviors* for life in the new society. From the visual and social media, food, and education to direct recruiting and marketing—some subtle, some blatant—all designed to rob the countries of their human capital resources and to acquire skills to shore up their own economies while making the process of integration into the new American environment less costly and smooth.

Thus, it appears to be an unwritten foreign policy strategy to use as many television programs as possible, even working through some Caribbean governments, to feed those would-be migrants with the American culture and societal norms, many of which became lethal to Caribbean cultural norms and practices.

The result is that a cadre of migrants has been created (with values) who look like, act like, dress like, and have the behavioral attitudes to guns and violence of normal inner-city Americans. Many develop disrespect for authority figures in the name of freedom and rights, aggressiveness to peers and adults, sexuality, and other tolerances observed in the American media. In addition, when any of these migrants get in trouble with the American justice system, they are required to serve their sentences and, invariably, are deported back to their home countries. Needless to say, the home Caribbean governments are ill equipped by law and any other means to deal with these "modern" issues for which their societies are not tailored.

It was in keeping with this background that a study was conducted to determine the impact and extent of this obviously visible "extended hand" of preparation.

All US Workers ages 16 and Over	*141,295*	*$32,000*
Native-Born Workers	119,095	$33,000
Immigrant Workers	22,200	$26,000
Black Immigrants	**1,962**	**$29,000**
Barbados	31	$36,000
Other West Indian countries	22	$35,000
Other Caribbean countries	10	$35,000
Antigua-Barbuda	11	$35,000
Grenada	19	$33,000
Jamaica	390	$32,000
Trinidad and Tobago	115	$32,000
St. Vincent	12	$32,000
St. Kitts-Nevis	8	$31,000
Bahamas	16	$30,000
Dominica	11	$30,000
St. Lucia	11	$27,000
Haiti	322	$25,000
Cuba	15	$24,000
Dominican Republic	52	$22,000

* Median annual earnings are for employed civilian workers with nonzero earnings only. Adults in the armed forces and those with negative or zero earnings are excluded.
Source; MPI analysis of 2005-2009 ACS, pooled.

Median estimated Caribbean household income in 2010

It is very widely accepted and known that Caribbean-born and Caribbean Americans and children of Caribbean nationals are making a contribution to the United States in a number of areas—including, but not confined to, politics, city administration, economics, culture, education, and medicine.

What is less clear is how Caribbean nationals here in the United States are impacting the development of their native land, especially in relation to the individual economies. According to the US Census in 2010, an estimated 4 million Caribbean nationals are residing in various parts of the United States. This figure includes nearly half from the English-speaking Caribbean countries.

CHAPTER 2

The Extent of Sociocultural Control

In a recent study this author attempted to examine the covert preparation and impact of the foreign sociocultural domination, assimilation, and the extent to which Caribbean peoples are in touch with events in their native countries, so to speak. This research consisted of *face-to-face* interaction and a *garbage analysis* of four major Caribbean communities—namely, but not exclusively, *Guyana, Barbados, Jamaica, and Trinidad and Tobago.* The methodology involved in phase 1 was to do interviews with store owners, families, school populations, and some non-Caribbean neighbors. The second phase of the study examined other economic issues and focused on a barrel trade, and the third phase examined the impact of repatriation of funds to the respective native countries.

The strategies and purposes in the preparation process focused on several factors, including how far-reaching the long arm of sociocultural preparation was on the behavior of the potential migrants at home and after migration and how deliberate is the process and the impact of the dominance on the native countries. Data was collected both in the original countries and in the United States, primarily in New York.

Phase 1

The objectives of this phase were to *examine the changing consumption patterns, music, and education in general, and to assess the impact of cultural and economic assimilation* that a dominant industrialized system imposes on a poor vulnerable one. In essence, to determine the extent to which such assimilation envelops the entire psyche of Caribbean peoples and separates them from their native countries. There is the prevailing belief that people become Americans long before they leave the shores of their native lands. This is indeed a function of the television programs and electronic technologies, the type of music and food that flood the local environment, the barrel trade, and the diaspora who return for short visits and tend to splurge with their American dollars / credit cards. In Guyana, there was even the notion that some people became Americans *just by reading the letters sent from their folks in the United States.*

There seems to be a covert, if not overt, attempt to continue the economic domination of these small states stymieing their expectations of economic independence, only this time, the colonials have different names. Coupled with this is the blatant and deliberate recruiting of Caribbean nationals to work in the United States. Recruiters were sent to offer incentives to persons just emerging from teachers' college, nursing schools, etc.

Political and academic interest in children, teenagers, and young adults preparing for future careers or exploring their options, and policies involving them, have increased in recent years. Caribbean governments, while essentially silent, seem to be keeping an open eye on many of the issues. Of particular concern is the impact foreign television programs and other media (news, commercials, and images) are having on the minds and, by definition, the behavior of their nationals. In addition to the imported products, whether through the barrel economy or other channels, two issues emerge: (a) the increased mental predisposition to things foreign, especially from the dominant United States culture, and (b) the way the local economies are being stagnated because of the preference for the foreign products. The latter, by its very scale of course, is so significant that it creates a negative impact on several sectors of the Caribbean economy.

Over the years, commentators have pointed to the phenomenon in song and other media. The Tradewinds, for example, refer to "Copycats" as those Caribbean nationals who become Yankees immediately after landing while a foreigner after spending ten years in the Caribbean still maintains his accent. The Mighty Cypher in his song "Fresh Water Yankee" asks the following:

> Born in this country
> Grow in this country
> Never left this country
> How come he tu'n Yankee?

Survey Analysis and Implications: Consumption Patterns

Of the 300 homes visited, the major food eaten based both on garbage residue and on interviews with the residents, 80% were of the fast-food variety, mainly Chinese, Italian, and American. There was very little evidence that native food was prepared in the homes, though these might have been purchased pre-prepared. Major indigenous food items were only prepared on special occasions and by adults 55 years old and above.

Caribbean-born persons between the ages of 15 and 25 years old who arrived in the United States within the last 5 years had already lost the taste or preference for native food items. The instances where such major food items were eaten, they may have been bought from restaurants and not prepared in the homes or, better yet, eaten at a friend's or relative's home. This reality (i.e., the apparent loss of taste for indigenous food items) seems to have been part of a process that began while the migrants were still in their native countries. Therefore, it was not only due to *the lack of knowledge of preparation* of the items in the homes but also the fact that "taste change" was influenced long before they arrived in the United States.

Within the last 10 years, there has been an increase in the franchise food businesses around Port of Spain, Bridgetown, Kingston, and Georgetown. The consumption of Taco Bell, Burger King, Wendy's, McDonald's, etc., as well as the beverages Pepsi and Coke, is changing the eating patterns of the societies. So the foreign influences on taste and consumption patterns that begin in the home countries for those Caribbean-born nationals which are passed on to their offspring, tend to become the basis of the eating and cooking approaches once they land. Fast-food mentality is therefore acquired and supported at the expense of the native food products even when these are readily available in the new communities.

During the investigation, there were 12 homes out of 115 that had working/ functioning stoves with pots and pans. All homes, however, had working microwave ovens.

The researchers found that there were at least 5 cases of children who took locally prepared items (e.g., boiled plantain and stew) in the lunch kit and were ridiculed by non-Caribbean students with little knowledge of the identity of the items. One little six-year-old girl refused to open her lunch kit to eat what her mother had prepared (i.e., boiled plantain and stew) and was returning the items untouched for several days before the parent found out the reason. When this child was given hamburger with chicken nuggets and fries, the problem was solved.

For many families with older children, the norm appears to be for parents to give students money to buy breakfast/lunch on the street and eat whatever is provided in school. (Opportunities where parents and their children sat around a table for any meal appeared to be few and far between.) When parents sit down to eat with the young ones, it was not at home but around a table in a fast-food place.

The periods of major preparation of food peculiar to the home countries were mainly during special occasions—e.g., Labor Day in Brooklyn, family backyard barbecues, various national independence celebrations, and when friends/ relatives visit from afar—that amounted to a total of 1 to 5 days per family per year. Even then, food was bought or brought in by the visitors/guests. Pressure of work and time and home space were cited as the main reasons why more cooking was not done in the homes.

The evidence suggests too that in most diets, native staples—such as ackee and salt fish, jerk meats, cocoa, oxtail preparations, mackerel rundown, green bananas, cow-foot and goat-head dishes, hard-dough bread and pastries, callaloo, flying fish, roti, curry, metem, pepper pot, soup, cook-up rice, and oil—either changed their "complexion" or were replaced by other food items including hamburgers, hotdogs, fries, Chinese food, spaghetti, tacos, pizza, and other items from the fast-food stores. Lack of preparation knowledge of the food from the original countries was especially significant among the fifteen- to twenty-five-year-old Caribbean-born groups and almost nonexistent in the US-born children of Caribbean parents.

The researchers asked about the presence of local-food preparation skills among both Caribbean-born residents between *17 to 24* and *25 to 40* years, and we were directed to the parents or an elderly relative within the home or away from the home who was usually depended on to prepare the authentic Caribbean dishes. All this in spite of the fact that in many predominantly Caribbean neighborhoods, the items used for such preparation are readily available in the community supermarkets. This suggests that the knowledge of the local "home food" preparation is slowly disappearing, and such preparation is being left to Sybil's, Sylvia's, Golden Krust, and other similar establishments. Consequently, wherever such knowledge exists in the home, the skill of food preparation is hardly being passed down to the young. For the younger children who just arrived, the consumption patterns were created before they arrived, and the preference for the "new food" did not begin when they arrived.

What is also significant is that in the Queens neighborhood of Richmond Hill, the data suggests that in the majority of homes, both Guyanese and Trinidadians, the traditional food is more often prepared. In fact, some of the same dietary and other cultural practices that existed in the native countries continued to be applied and adhered to in many homes, mostly in Indo-Guyanese and Trinidadian homes. This was corroborated by the store/supermarket managers who indicated that daily sales of fish types (e.g., *gilbakker, bangamary, salted fish, codfish, shrimp, butter fish, hassar,* and *pattwa*) and vegetables (e.g., *bhagee, corrila, byghan, ochro, bora, sijan, callaloo,* etc.) have remained very high due to the demand from residents.

During the interviews, only 2% of Caribbean-born residents between 14 and 19 years old who came to the United States within the last 5 years could name 5 food products native to their countries and could not remember how many times those items were prepared in the homes. Among those Caribbean-born between 21 and 45 who were residents for 5 to 10 years, the percentage increased to 63%.

The conclusion from the garbage analysis and the subsequent household interviews was twofold. Most of the dietary items consumed by resident US Caribbean nationals were unlikely to constitute the major dietary items that would have been prepared in their original respective countries. Secondly, the data suggests that those Caribbean-born residents who came within 1 to 15 years appear to have acquired many of the new dietary tastes before arriving in the United States. In addition, the US-born Caribbean residents were not exposed enough to many of the traditional foods in the new country, if any at all, and therefore were less familiar with the cuisine of their parents' birth countries.

Phase 2

In 2012, we asked Caribbean-born residents between the ages of *15 to 25* and *26 to 60* questions related to their general knowledge of the Caribbean to see the extent to which they or their parents were keeping up with the events in their native countries or the region as a whole or, at best, could recall those events after or before they migrated.

The same questions were put to residents of both age categories. The following is a sample of the questions asked and the responses:

1. Name the three Caribbean nationals who won the Nobel Prize and the countries they are from.

    There was *no correct* answer from the first age group (15-25), and *five* persons from the second group (26-60) got one name correct. In five homes, which were outside the target countries, the respondents could not even recall the person from their own country.

2. Give the names of five current Caribbean political leaders / prime ministers or president.

    In the first group, 15% got two correct answers while 41% of the second group got three correct. No one was able to name any five political leaders. There were fifteen examples where the respondents did not know the present leaders of their own countries.

3. What does the term CARICOM mean?

    Of 100 students in the first age group who were asked this question, 55% answered correctly, while in the second age group, the correct response topped 88% of the 205 persons questioned.

4. Give the names of any five Caribbean writers.

    In the first age group, 1% named one writer, and in the second age group, 35% remembered two writers. No one in either group was able to come up with the names of any five Caribbean writers.

5. Name any five singers/entertainers from the Caribbean.

The response to this question was much better than expected. In the first age group, 60% of the residents surveyed named five, 32% named four, and the rest came up with two entertainers. In the second age group, 90% of the respondents were able to name five singers/entertainers, mainly reggae and calypso personalities.

6. Name any five famous Caribbean sports personalities/performers.

This proved to be also an easy question to answer and generated over 90% responses and correct answers. However, the respondents tended to name cricketers mainly from their own countries, except Jamaicans who were able to identify noncricket sports personalities (e.g., athletes).

7. Can you list any five Caribbean capital cities?

This question proved more difficult for both groups than was anticipated. While 90% of group 1 and 95% of group 2 remembered four capital cities, the fifth one seemed to have eluded many respondents. The four cities that were correctly identified were in Barbados, Trinidad, Jamaica, and Guyana.

A sampling of the comment/observation sections of CXC examinations on candidates' answers seems to confirm many of these *responses*.

In one of the comments (May/June 2010, Caribbean history), the following were noted:

And candidates could have mentioned enhanced political consciousness, demand for greater sociopolitical freedoms . . . From the responses it became clear that the candidates possessed little knowledge of the question.

Candidates appeared not to have had and extensive knowledge of this topic.

Candidates ignored the guidelines and displayed knowledge pertinent to other areas of the topic. Overall many candidates appeared to be deficient in the detailed knowledge that was required.

8. Another question in the study was related to *career choices* among Caribbean-born residents ages 12 to 17 living in the United States between 1 and 5 years. These residents were asked to list their career choices in order of preference. The results of the study revealed the following:

Medicine	0.5%
Law	0.1%
Sports (basketball)	35.0%
Music (rapper/singer)	57.0%
Science/technology	0.2%
Education	2.0%
Politics	0.2%
Unsure	5.0%

Of the respondents, 95% indicated that the career determination was made before they left their homeland.

It should be observed that none of the top two sports or music choices included any major (except athletics) Caribbean activity (e.g., cricket, football [soccer], or reggae).

The expectation here was that coming from the Caribbean, newly arrived residents would have career choices relevant to their native communities and not to the countries to which they were destined. It shows more directly the extent to which their minds were already influenced by their education, especially through the media.

It seems that many of the sources of the questionable responses offered by respondents reflect and extend to the quality of education being offered at primary and secondary levels in the home countries. The report from the civil society in Guyana in the National Development Strategy (May 2000) summarizes the problems as follows:

> A number of economic and social factors . . . have led to a most unsatisfactory and unacceptable state of affairs: learning rates in the schools are extremely low; a proportion of the teaching force is unqualified and untrained, absenteeism on the part of both teachers and students; and textbooks and other instructional materials are often unavailable.

> Guyana's success in attaining universal access to primary schools . . . has been eroded and has been replaced by rising repetition and dropout rates. Moreover [there are] alarmingly high levels of functional illiteracy and questionable broad based education.

Further, the report argues that primary education does not provide enough current events and the education being offered by the community and high schools is inadequate. Functional literacy for young adults, the report warned, is not likely even at the tertiary level.

The report obviously recognized the other problem in the equation in concluding that "in addition to the bleak scenario described above, is the debilitating hemorrhage of qualified experienced teachers to the Caribbean, North America and even Africa."

It is troubling to observe that after spending much-needed, scarce resources to train teachers, nurses, Medex, and industrial technicians, recruiters from countries that contribute nothing to these training programs turn up offering incentives and grabbing these trained personnel to fill the gaps in their own economies.

Small regions such as the Caribbean have to view this as a troubling development. Already, more than 80% of tertiary-educated people of Jamaica and Guyana work in industrialized countries, including the United States. The figures are in excess of 60% for Trinidad and Tobago and Surinam, and the numbers are unacceptably high for countries such as Antigua and Barbuda, Saint Kitts and Nevis, and Saint Lucia.

It is very depressing that states in the Caribbean pay heavily to educate and train their own people for their own economic and sociocultural development only to lose them to the international industrial market. The so-called first world countries are attracting the cream of skills from the so-called third world countries with no compensation. It's not only the United States' green card attraction but recently, Europe is getting into the fray with their own blue card motivation to fulfill their lack of sufficiently skilled workers in both their private and public sectors.

The entire practice reflects an urgent need for small countries, especially in the Caribbean, to bring to the attention of the international organizations the disaster that is being created. Postindependence Caribbean countries suffered from the hardships created when they had to pay high costs to IMF and other lending bodies to sustain and improve their economies. In fact, some became more dependent on the "aid" that was offered. Now, they are being drained of their very lifeblood at a rate that will delay considerably, if not destroy, their infrastructure. Industrial countries should be made to pay recruitment fees for the skills that they are poaching.

However, there is the political will to initiate strategies that would halt and hopefully reverse these trends.

Caribbean countries—especially Guyana, Trinidad, Jamaica, and Barbados—have been the target of recruitment by North America. Indeed, they had produced an overabundance of teachers and nurses, in addition to other skills, that we are willing to turn a blind eye to these strategies. In fact, one island even encouraged certain qualified categories to migrate in the hope of earning reciprocate remittance.

Now, we get this statement from the government of Guyana:

> Government has signaled its intentions to hire Math and Science teachers from abroad and is even considering retaining those that are of retirement age.

There has always been the belief that in a postcolonial Caribbean society, the continued dependence on and influence of the dominant cultures and economies will decrease. Nowhere have these influences been observed than in the education system, both in context and content. The comments of the Caribbean Examination Council examiners while commending excellent performances from some students continue to refer to the following:

> Candidates experienced some difficulty in producing the answer that was required. (question 11, GP June 2010)

Overall many candidates appeared to be deficient in the detailed knowledge that was required for this question. (question 12, GP June 2010)

Candidates lacked the required knowledge base for this question.

In addition the responses [to this question] required the application of reasoning and analytical skills and too many candidates suffered adversely not for want of knowledge but for the application of these skills.

In a decade of observable declining local resource industries and an obvious struggle for foreign capital resources, attention continues to be focused on the Caribbean diaspora for direct and indirect support. Governments continue to lament the flight of not only their human resources but also financial resources to foreign countries. Some countries had been trying for years to control this flight or even stop it. In both situations, the attempts have proven futile.

CHAPTER 3

Returning Resources and Remittances

Phase 3

Evidence from the 200 barrels examined in the study shows that the contents were distributed as follows: food items (canned/packaged goods, candy, cheese) make up 40.5%, items of clothing (male, female, baby, and school items) 32%, varied electronic-based items 10.5%, and miscellaneous items (spare parts, cables, gadgets, games, and toys) 18%. The average cost of preparing a barrel was indicated as between $100 and $200 while the cost of mailing varied between $80 and $110 per barrel, depending on size and quality.

According to the US Department of Commerce, in 2008, the total cost of this trade to the Caribbean region was US$5 billion. Guyana received a total of between US$40 and US$60 million of barrel items from the United States alone within the year. Figures for Canada and the UK were not immediately available. The obvious question that arises is, what was the impact of this inflow on the economy?

It has been argued that the answer to this question is twofold.

Many emerging industries in these countries either have failed or are struggling badly. Take the garment industry as an example. If hundreds of thousands of dollars were being spent on purchasing items of clothing in foreign countries to send to the Caribbean, this would obviously impact on the local garment industry. If a Guyanese prefers a shirt manufactured in the United States, whether it is sent in a barrel or he buys it from money sent to him from a relative, whose economy is he supporting? It seems that the local shirt industry has to compete uncomfortably with this trade, and the resultant loss of employment and productive activity cannot be good for the local economy.

There was and still is the belief strongly held by many in the entire Caribbean that foreign products are better, more durable, and by definition, much more fashionable than those manufactured locally. This notion not only continues to fuel this particular trade but also seems to drive the thinking and spirit of an entire society. Some decision makers felt that with political independence, such beliefs would disappear. However, not only did it remain; the nations also continue to look outside for solutions to crime, industrial unrest, industrial identification and development, and research and resource allocation, to name a few.

This preference for foreign products is not a new phenomenon. In the 1980s, the late Forbes Burnham, Guyana's president and leader of the PNC government, took measures to ban imported food commodities, even against the prevailing public opinion. Not only that, but Burnham also proceeded to embark on a campaign to grow more and eat more locally produced goods. His "Be local, buy local campaign" was aimed at changing the taste of Guyanese from foreign commodities. The basis of his thesis was not only economic; he posited that foreign goods and services were also being used as tools to maintain sociocultural and political dependency. Burnham used local expertise for development wherever they could be found. He even repatriated skilled Guyanese living abroad by offering them attractive foreign exchange contract packages in his belief that local expertise must be tapped first before looking elsewhere. Many scholars have argued that Burnham must have lived way before his time.

Apart from stymieing the development and growth of industries that manufacture some of the products that are contained in barrels, the trade is obviously preventing much-wider opportunities for employment, wage earning, and a much-better, evenly spread quality of life: US$40 million worth.

Most of the persons interviewed expressed the view that they never thought of it this way. In fact, they offered two reasons why they send the items:

1. To provide some sustenance for their relatives and friends who cannot do so for themselves (i.e., scarce and/or expensive food items), 55% responded.

2. To provide a source of income (through street merchandizing) and employment, 46% responded.

They never wanted the items to be used in a manner to suggest that they were scrounging off their overseas relatives (showing off) or living freely. However, the arrival of a barrel was an occasion of great anticipation, joy, and showing off on their less fortunate neighbors and friends. There is always an element of magic, sophistication, and even reverence about things and people that come from foreign countries, even if these can be readily obtained locally.

In the article "Systemic Caribbean Dependency," *Michael Roberts* notes the degree of dependence of CARICOM governments on their nationals abroad, especially in the United States. According to Roberts, "[Hard cash] remittances is another billion dollar industry that while important from a position of poverty and need has helped to facilitate negative aspects of Cultural Imperialism in the Caribbean."

Roberts asserts that this (barrel) industry "is supported here in the United States by poor, working-class Caribbean immigrants who send food and clothing to loved ones back home in various sizes of barrels. It has spawned a proliferation of shipping companies and helped transfer changes in diet and deepened the dependence on US consumer products."

Roberts further contends that "aided and abetted by a constant, unrelenting flow of US television commercials, advertising of clothes, foods, underwear, shoes, and other consumer products, Caribbean nationals have now developed a morbid fixation with things American in the minds of people living in the Caribbean . . . Things manufactured and made in the region are seen as inferior and at any rate are more expensive than those allegedly made in America although most of these foods [products] were manufactured in China, Japan, Singapore, and Taiwan."

Roberts concludes that "from food to clothes to the latest movies and digital gadgetry Caribbean people, especially the youths, hunger for American products. These find their way in barrels and on on-line shopping web-sites. Nowadays the apparel choices of people in the Caribbean are no different to that of East New York of Harlem. As a matter of fact the youths in the

Caribbean now identify more readily with hip-hop and gangsta rap than with indigenous reggae or calypso—so invasive is this cultural imperialism and domination."

In many instances, the poor work three jobs, denying themselves some of the basic necessities of economic advancement in order to provide for the folks back home or even get into debt to impress their folks and show that they are doing so well in the United States.

Remittances

At a time when Caribbean nations are continuing to feel the effects of the global economic slowdown and the impact of the financial crisis due to a slide in spending by tourists, high inflation, and escalating joblessness, remittances from the diaspora may turn out to be a financial lifeline—a silver lining (Best 2010). Except that many in this diaspora who have lost their jobs or had to find lower-paying jobs find themselves contributing much less than previously, if any at all.

Remittances generally reduce the severity of poverty and frequently lead to a higher accumulation of human capital, higher health and education expenditures, better access to information and communication technologies, greater financial access, small-business investments, and entrepreneurship expansion.

The World Bank believes optimistically that the flow of money to families in the Caribbean from relatives living in the United States, Canada, Britain, and elsewhere may increase by about 25% during the next 3 years.

Country	2007	2008	2009	2010
Jamaica	2.14B	1.80B	1.90B	2.00B
Barbados	147M	168M	149M	161M
Guyana	283M	278M	253M	280M
Trinidad	NA	109M	99M	109M

According to World Bank estimates in 2010, a quarter of Guyana's GDP consisted of emigrant remittances. The report argued that as increasing numbers of Guyanese leave their country to live elsewhere, "the money they sent back home is playing a growing role in the country's economy."

"The amount of remittance to Guyana increased more than eight times between 2007 and 2010 going from US$27 million to US$218 million." The Inter-American Development Bank's report of 2007 stated that the total of all remittances (money transfers) to Latin America and the Caribbean in 2005 was US$ billion. This money came mainly from the United States, Canada, Europe, and Japan, and it came in small amounts of between US$50 and US$300.

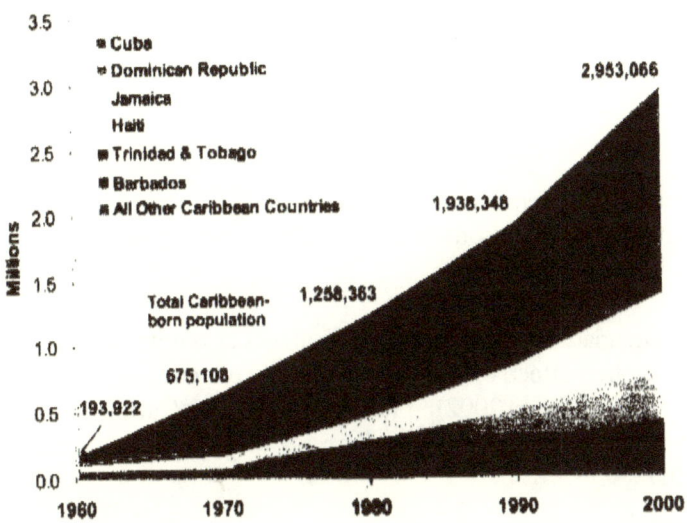

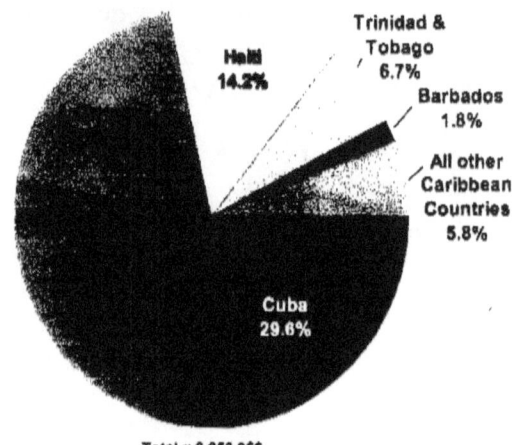

Trinidad &
Tobago
6.7%

Haiti
14.2%

Barbados
1.8%

All other
Caribbean
Countries
5.8%

Cuba
29.6%

Total = 2,953,066

Note: Other Caribbean countries includes those reporting their birthplace as
Dominica, St. Lucia, St. Kitts-Nevis, Montserrat, Aruba, the Netherlands Antilles,
the Cayman Islands, the British Virgin Islands, Guadeloupe, Turks and Calcos
Islands, Martinique, Anguilla, the West Indies, and St. Barthelemy.
Source: US Census Bureau, Census 2000.

Because most of the remittances go directly to the immigrant households that have a high propensity to consume, the multiplier effect of a country's national income can be considerable.

A study in Bangladesh, for example, indicates that remittances to that country have a multiplier effect of 3.3 on GNP, 2.8 on consumption, and 0.4 on investment (van Doorn 2002). The figures for the Caribbean countries are believed to be much higher given the ratio of population to the number of immigrants.

Another study looking at the relationship between poverty, migration, and remittances for 74 low—and middle-income developing countries found that both international migration and remittances have a strong statistically significant impact on reducing poverty in the developing world.

In a study on Latin America and the Caribbean, it was found that remittances put large sums of money into circulation in countries in Latin America and the Caribbean for the purchase of goods and services that boost the economy. In this way, remittance flows have a positive effect on economic development (Rhyme 2007).

In another study in Inter-American Dialogue (2007, page 15), it was observed that remittances are improving the lives of poor families and communities in most recipient countries—particularly those in which migrant senders came from the poorest groups.

Based on the studies that have been conducted on the impact of remittances, some policy issues are being addressed. One major issue is the attempt by some countries to lower the costs of remittance transfers. Some negotiations between countries and the transfer companies have not gone too well, while others have made some progress. Western Union, MoneyGram, and others have generally high and regressive rates of transfer, which tend to interfere with the quantity of remittance transferred.

Another issue is the remittances that do not go through the official transfer process (i.e., undeclared movement of moneys through travel). This source, it is estimated, adds another 50% to the total.

Migrants who do not return but attract their families to them or set up families of their own in their new environments tend to reduce the remittances sent or cut it out altogether, maintaining two households in the process.

Considering that between Guyana, Trinidad, and Jamaica, over 25,000 nationals migrate every year. *Dr. Ngozi Okonjo-Iweala* (2011) urges the Caribbean government to tap more into their diaspora. She contends that "diaspora *bonds* are an innovative instrument to mobilize the diaspora's savings" for national development. She noted that Caribbean countries receive the equivalent of 7% of their GDP in remittances every year, with Jamaica alone accounting for 1 million or more nationals abroad who send home nearly $2 billion in remittances annually. "These Jamaicans may not be wealthy, but because of their number, significant amounts of development funding could be raised." The same argument could be applied to other Caribbean countries. Caribbean nationals, Okonjo-Iweala argues. These countries could be encouraged to invest in small sums in purchasing structured market bonds that could operate like regular bounds and could be bought and sold by government and private companies and public/private partnerships to Caribbeans living abroad.

Why, therefore, is there then the paucity of development funding and the obvious lack of projects supporting employment in these countries? The arrow seems to point to poor management and its accompanying twin partner, corruption, discussed earlier.

It should be noted too that several reports identified the sacrifices being made by the diaspora in working two and three jobs in order to send remittances back home. Some of these pay rent and travel on public transportation in order to provide a comfortable (sometimes the best) living and more than "idle" existence for those in the home country, even if it means using their credit cards (borrowing). How sad!

According to Bernard (2012), some very interesting scenarios are noticeable. This writer observes that in Guyana particularly and in the Caribbean generally, businesses in the region have shifted to importation rather than designing and manufacturing goods and services to address the needs of their local people. Countries are becoming less creative and innovative. In addition, Bernard notes, young people are less inclined to or interested in serious education themselves because of the lack of opportunities, coupled with the fact that "stuff" comes from overseas regularly. The obvious signs in these countries of prosperity and high standard of living are, in fact, a facade. These lifestyles are being constantly supported with funds from abroad and are very vulnerable to recessions in the United States and elsewhere.

Sociologists have observed that there are higher-than-normal rates of poverty, divorces, crime, spousal abuse, alcoholism, illicit drug use, gang membership, and lack of upward mobility among Caribbean people living in communities in the United States. Eventually, some end up on welfare with mental health issues. No wonder a practice of some of residents is cheating or trying to cheat the landlords of rent for substandard basement dwellings. Eating fish heads, chicken feet, pork trotters, cow skin, and heels has moved from cultural practice to economic necessity among quite a few. As a result, labels like poor and low income have surfaced, and in some cases, people have been marginalized, not getting business loans and other financial support needed for growth.

CHAPTER 4

Migration and Control

It does not seem to be a conscious effort on the part of many to deliberately contribute to the "development" of their country once they are in the United States. It is, however, indisputable that they desire to better their own educational, economical, and financial situation by migrating overseas. The effort in providing for family and friends back home has the unintended consequence of contributing to national development through spending, taxes, small-business development, and other benefits. According to the data, this is not altogether true, for many who arrive are already educated.

The Caribbean region has seen significant numbers of its citizens emigrate. The migration rate of the college-educated people in the Caribbean is among the highest in the world. It is estimated that about 79% of Jamaicans, for example, with a college education or below live in the United States. Until a few years ago, the so-called brain drain was considered to be a net loss for poor countries like those in the Caribbean. However, some of these countries' governments have been utilizing the skills, training, and resources of the diaspora communities to counteract the negative economic and other consequences of the "loss."

Accordingly, Percy Hintzen of the University of California at Berkeley argues that because of their "well educated diasporas Caribbean nations can, like China and India, take advantage of the trend of outsourcing high skilled jobs" in reverse. First, they will have to attract some of the educated diaspora back into their home country. To do so, according to Hintzen, these governments must first develop an organized plan of community contact through their embassies, consulates, and other overseas-based organizations. In addition, they should also establish offices dedicated to diaspora affairs to identify and channel human and material resources back to their home countries.

Such actions, Hintzen argues, will further the diaspora's participation in the home country's development. In addition, Hintzen contends that Caribbean governments can offer incentives to their emigrant populations to facilitate visits and retirement in the home country. In turn, members of the diaspora can use their acquired skills to work on projects in the home countries, such as training, management, and implementation.

Top Emigration Caribbean Countries by Tertiary Education, 2000

	Number of Migrants (Thousands)
Guyana	89.0
Grenada	85.1
Jamaica	85.1
St. Vincent and the Grenadines	84.5
Haiti	83.6
Trinidad and Tobago	79.3
St. Kitts and Nevis	78.5
St. Lucia	71.1
Antigua and Barbuda	66.8
Belize	65.5
Dominica	64.2
Bahamas	61.3
Surinam	47.9

It is estimated that there are over 3 million people from the Caribbean (2000 census) currently living in the United States, although evidence from the 2010 census suggests that there has been a 6% migration reduction. This is equivalent to about 1% of the total population. The major reasons advanced for this migration, according to scholars, are the desire to advance the education opportunities for themselves and their families. Closely connected to this is the desire to create and sustain an increasing economic foundation. In some situations, political and civil strife within their native countries tend to "push" a sizable number of residents out to seek peace and stability. These push factors also included inadequate enumeration and benefits, unfavorable working conditions, insufficient career opportunities, and deteriorating living and working conditions. So desperate were people to leave their countries that members of touring teams of soccer players and musicians and other performers passing through airports in the United States would simply disappear.

Within the last 20 years, however, the "pull/push" migration factors gained strength. Given the growing need for certain professionals in the United States and other countries, recruiters were sent out to Guyana and other states of the Caribbean to secure the skills of nurses and teachers, medical workers, hotel workers, sports performers, etc.

The Caribbean has been experiencing increasing waves of recruitment targeted at their skilled human resources and students. These practices usually begin at the local level through the increasingly developing Internet applications, advertisements, and inducements published in the local media. Once applications are received, the interviews and the recruitment sessions are arranged at local centers. The real motivational force for this movement of peoples from these nations seems to be related to the region's underdevelopment compared to Europe and North America. The single most important reason then for the tradition of migration that has become an intrinsic aspect of the life in the Caribbean is the search abroad for a better quality of life than what was being enjoyed in all the region's economically troubled nations.

There is evidence to suggest that some government personnel in some countries are involved in the process. The most popular recruiting countries continue to be the United Kingdom, Canada, and the United States, with most recruits preferring the latter country. The following examples of Jamaica are typical of a deliberate policy aimed at the Caribbean and other countries.

An example for nurses in a Jamaican newspaper reads thus:

Registered Nurses—Florida US

> Salary from US36K-US50K per annum, no state taxes. Permanent Visa processing at no cost for nurse who passes an interview with our Florida Hospital Clients . . . Also we need Registered Pharmacists. Starting salary for Pharmacists is US60K+ . . . Call for schedule of local interview soon. (*The Gleaner*, November 19, 2000, 123F)

In addition, visiting teams of recruiters assisted by local institutions and individuals help to recruit local skills by organizing recruitment fairs in individual islands, and the recruitment visits are advertised in the local press and media. Many of these events will attract hundreds, if not thousands, seeking the opportunity to migrate. In one event in September 2001, more than 35,000 Jamaicans flocked to a center where more than 40 American, Canadian, and United Kingdom personnel were seeking to recruit students and other personnel. Even the US secretary of state, while making some comments on International Education Week in 2001, remarked that "international students enrich American communities with their academic abilities and cultural diversity" (*The Sunday Gleaner*, September 9, 2001, 11C).

The attractive packages offered were often difficult to refuse. Large numbers of the professionals therefore left (in most cases, immediately after training) to work overseas, and most never returned to their native countries. Even when looked upon as a positive development in terms of the transfer of goods and money, the net effect of skill migration is to create a shortage of the skills from the native countries, especially considering the scarce resources used to train them in the first place. In both Trinidad and Tobago and Guyana, the deteriorating health and education services were directly related to these factors.

It is not clear whether one condition would make up for the other, but a closer examination of the activities (as emerged from the study) suggest that the economic and sociocultural impact must be telling indeed. In terms of numbers, an IMF working paper in 2006 suggested that approximately 12% of the labor force of the Caribbean migrated to the developed countries between 1965 and 2000. This compares to 7% from Central America, the second source of migrants, and less than 2% from East and South Central Asia during the same period. Further, an average 70% of the tertiary labor force and 42% of the secondary labor force have left their native Caribbean countries. In terms of the former, Grenada, Guyana, Haiti, Jamaica, and Saint Vincent have record migration rates above 80%, with 61% tertiary levels and 3% secondary levels settling in the United States.

Cumulative Impact of Migration on the Native Countries

In order to get around many of the obstacles—economic, and political, which exist—families have been trying to migrate one by one. A parent might migrate first, hoping to settle down, work, and be able to send for the others left behind. Of course, this has resulted in a number of socioeconomic and sociological problems. During the last 10 years, 30% of the migrants were "piece" arrivals (part of a family, usually a parent who eventually sends for the rest of the family members). Of this number, only 5% reunited successfully. While here, the arriving parent established new family relationships and never sent for members of his/her original family. The breakdown per territory shows the following:

Top Emigration Caribbean Countries in 2010
(as percentage of their population)

Grenada	65.5
St. Kitts and Nevis	61.0
Guyana	56.8
Antigua and Barbuda	48.3
Barbados	41.0
Surinam	39.0
St. Vincent and the Grenadines	37.6
Jamaica	36.1
Trinidad and Tobago	26.7
St. Lucia	23.2

(Source: *Migration and Remittances Factbook 2011*)

Economic Contributions of West Indians
to Their Home Countries

There is no doubt that remittances play a pivotal role in the development of Caribbean countries. So significant that the practice is encouraged both from the standpoint of making the immigration process fast and accommodating and also making the transfer of funds easy. Some of the internal activities in individual home countries that are supported by and that have become dependent on remittances from the diaspora include the following:

a. Construction and renovation of homes and other buildings for self and family members as vacation accommodation or for the day of permanent return

b. Providing materials and equipment for education and computer training (i.e., acquiring space for such)

c. Establishing "trading" contact with friends and family to set up roadside or in-mall vendor / retail stores

d. Providing support for village and community development activities through third parties

e. Purchasing and owning businesses that sell electrical and security systems

f. Purchasing and providing spare parts for passenger transportation business (taxis and minibuses) and other commercial ventures

g. Providing material and/or completed costumes for cultural and national celebrations (e.g., carnival festivities)

All these activities have given rise to lucrative shipping companies as well as money-transfer businesses. Other services include pension / social security transfers and making US currency available for foreign transactions (see "Systemic Caribbean Dependency" in OPEdNews).

The Caribbean Diaspora: Sacrifices and Reality

The picture that emerges is not all positive in relation to the triple concepts of the migration, remittances, and development in the Caribbean.

While evidence suggests that remittances have and are continuing to add and aid development in their home countries, some writers have suggested evidence that shows a negative impact on the individual psyche. *Keith Bernard* (2007), for example, argues that "remittances have shifted the responsibility of the Guyanese Government and business to provide employment and other public goods," the implication being that the barrel economy and remittances are filling the holes and moving the economy from manufacturing and designing to importation. In addition, Bernard asserts that the Guyanese citizens have become so complacent and content that they are not "pressuring the government to create jobs and better public services." With the flow of goods, the population is losing whatever self-sufficiency, motivation, and innovation the Burnham government tried to inculcate.

Secondly, there is evidence to suggest that the diaspora who save and send resources in the barrels and remittances consists of folks who work two and three jobs, pay rent, and ride the public transportation in all kinds of weather to provide a more-than-comfortable existence for their folks in their native countries. The evidence also suggests that while "the well to do Caribbean diaspora" is responsible for a mere 13% of the repatriated resource, the not so well-off are responsible for 87% of such support.

CHAPTER 5

The Global Economic Issues and the Caribbean

In "Financial Crisis: Dilemma or Opportunity for Caribbean Diaspora," Curtis Ward (2011) argues that the impact of the global financial crisis has hit the Caribbean diaspora extremely hard at a time when the need for finance is greatest. Since remittances from the diaspora contribute significantly to the GDP of all Caribbean countries, development plans and progress have had to be reexamined. In some countries, the drop in remittances could be as high as 20% or between US$400 million and US$5 billion a year in foreign exchange earnings. This immediately affects the ability to purchase goods and services from abroad and reduce the countries' ability to finance their external obligations.

In addition, this reduction of remittances will likely have a multiplier effect on the internal socioeconomics of the countries. Purchasing power and consumption patterns referred to earlier will have to be adjusted, at best, to cope. The very income, production, and acquisition of resources and the receptivity of market forces for fishermen, builders, local shopkeepers, and vendors are likely to be adversely affected.

Coupled with all these are other reduced benefits that seem less noticeable but are no less significant. The diaspora's ability to travel back and forth between their countries could be severely limited. High airfares, job layoffs, and credit squeezes may make such travel become less frequent.

The impact of the dominant culture has been used to explain why so many migrants are arriving with behaviors and expectations consistent with their new environment and a diminished knowledge of the country from which they came. In many Caribbean countries, the increasing urge to think foreign is being reinstated not only by television but also by foreign food and other business operations. These operations impose foreign tastes, style, and socioeconomic behaviors on vulnerable emerging nations.

It seems that the education system ought to place a greater scope and emphasis on local and regional studies, especially in areas of current political developments and economic practices, in addition to sociocultural trends and activities.

The Caribbean community, it seems, is a constantly developing and dynamic experience, and its citizens of all ages need to be aware of what is taking place. In addition to the education system, the public information system, including the local and regional media, has a major role to play in the dissemination of knowledge and to encourage debate on the issues as they develop. Local and regional governments cannot allow their countries to be enveloped by big-country power and influence, or else, the whole practice of political and economic independence would have been nullified.

Michael Roberts (2007) sums the situation this way. He asserts that

> it is safe to say that even as Caricom [Caribbean Community] shouts its independence in 2007 to the world the very things that make the region truly Caribbean are now under siege and independence have thus become and relegated to a territory.

He further asserts that

> a look at the economics of the region helps to reinforce the neo-dependency vehicle that distorts warps and stultifies the growth of the region without the historically crude use of guns and threats.

The obverse side to all this is that, as has been already alluded, the migrants seem to be prepared early to serve in the destination countries. Many scholars believe that these migrants contribute to economic growth in numerous ways. They refer to the filling of labor market needs in high-skill and low-skill segments of the market, rejuvenating populations, improving labor market efficiency, promoting entrepreneurship, spurring urban renewal, and injecting dynamism and diversity into destination countries and societies.

In previous cases, the process of integration of newcomers took time and presented many negative issues for the receiving countries.

Immigrants tend to face many natural barriers when they first arrive, but the sociocultural difference between them and the rest of the society tend to narrow over time. It is this transition period that the dominant culture is trying to shorten and making less severe on its economy.

It is clear that one of the major intentions of the developed economies is the preparation of the potential migrants early for integration into their new societies so that less effort and financial burdens will be incurred. In addition, this would begin their contribution to their new society immediately upon arrival. The smooth interaction between newcomers and their host communities seem of particular importance to both groups if measurable economic, social, and political benefits are to accrue.

Policies that some governments are considering and have considered include return migration. It seems that the constant draining of skills and the breaking up of the social/economic structure has been seen as more significant than the repatriation of remittances. Many migrants have returned voluntarily after a short stay in the destination countries. In this way, migration rarely represents a total displacement of migrants from the home country on the outward move or from the destination country on the return. The thing is that most migrants are part of a transnational system of outward movements and reciprocal flows of capital—economic, social, as well as human.

However, this transnational nature of the migrants' livelihoods also facilitates their remaining at the destination while supporting the household at home and being involved with many aspects of family life without actually returning to work and live in the Caribbean.

Efforts to attract expatriates with skills to return are being made by and in some Caribbean countries. Some countries (e.g., Jamaica and Guyana) have established a Returning Residents Program aimed at encouraging the return of nationals from abroad through public information in the countries that have major concentrations of their nationals. The plan also consisted of offering tax concessions on the importation of household goods, settling-in allowance, and air transportation. In Guyana, the "back home call" ran into a number of problems when returnees were offered salary and allowances in US dollars and conveniences no less favorable than what they enjoyed in the departing countries.

The time in the migration cycle at which the return is encouraged is very important. A five-year period of living abroad is estimated to be optimal for the return of skilled nationals. It seems that this period will allow for their graduating with their particular skill and fulfilling their immigration requirements. Of course, it all depends on the migrant's educational level at the time of the migration.

SOME CONCLUDING OBSERVATIONS

Many Caribbean economists including Lewis since (1954) theorized very early that the process of growth in the Caribbean economy would follow a methodical approach. That was colonial Caribbean. The popular concept then was that agriculture and land alone would constrain growth and only state policies and capital accumulation would generate jobs, lower unemployment rates, raise output for export both regionally and extra regionally.

It was not perceived that post-independence Caribbean would run into this level and monster of designed economic and cultural control.

The most frightening aspect of these developments which have emerged, points to the fact that the Caribbean is definitely losing the battle for growth and development and the retention of its own skills.

It is further alarming that Caribbean States which fought hard and long for political independence from the colonial masters have moved from colonial dependency to post-colonial dependence and control in every vital national area. It has become a joke for Caribbean leaders to even whisper anything sounding like integration. Constant barriers and opposition are being established against the free movement of Caribbean peoples between states and the continued bugbear of insularity is ever present. Carifta and Caricom were not intended nor did they help to solve the apparent disdain and suspicions that one set of Caribbean people have for another. Just listen to the speeches or stand at a port of entry and observe the behaviors. Indeed while this continues to exist poverty and dependency parade themselves as economic progress.

Many of the issues highlighted in this analysis need to be addressed by the Caribbean leadership urgently or risk the national embarrassment of sliding backwards to a position worse than the first.

Some economists and financial experts have opined that remittances in whatever form cannot sustain Caribbean economies for any length of time, nor can this practice compensate for the flight of skills which is taking place.

Without one voice and a consolidated union, small nations become easy prey to multinationals and rich developed ones. These poor countries are being used as suppliers of skills for the rich countries and to fill their economic needs. The preparation for life abroad is done in the home countries under the very noses of the political governments and facilitates easy integration into their new environment. Scarce resources are spent by these countries to train personnel for their own purposes and then have to lose them to deliberate skills poaching. So while the economies of the Caribbean remain stuck it is the rich countries which are sucking their lifeblood. Already some Caribbean governments are forced to import 'cheap' labor from China and other places to meet their specific labor needs—a task which seems to be creating more domestic problems than it solves.

What is clear also is that some Caribbean governments not only see remittances as positive outcomes but seek to rely heavily on their diaspora. While doing this they ignore the bigger problems and allow their peoples to be so transformed. In the meantime it is the diaspora who are financing the development or lack thereof of some of these states—a situation in which only the rich countries would benefit and the poor underdeveloped countries remain tagged with the 'underdeveloped' pseudonym.

Despite the losses however some scholars see many positives. They see migration as a means whereby people can extend their opportunities and gain experience in an international setting then returning to apply those skills to their homeland. Of course some constraints have to be put in place to harness the bleeding and limit it to nationally acceptable levels. What these levels are will vary from island to island. With the paucity of relevant data research on this issue will take some time.

In the meantime this economic shock has to be absorbed by the states by encouraging remigration on a very sizeable and organized scale and in targeted areas. No economic domestic and foreign strategy will be successful however without Caribbean Governments approaching them with collaboration and trust among the various peoples something which is woefully lacking at present.

APPENDIX

International Migration

Total immigrants[a]	11,599
Total refugees[a]	..
Total emigrants[b]	417,469
Skilled emigration rate, tertiary educated[c]	85.9%
Average annual net migration[d]	-8,000

Notes: [a]2010; [b]2005; [c]2000; [d]2005-2010

Sources: International Migrant Stock, 2009
World Population Prospects, 2008
Migration and Remittances Factbook, 2008

Selected Socioeconomic Indicators

Total population[a]	752,940
Annual population growth[a]	-0.63%
Life expectancy at birth[a]	66.31
Infant mortality rate (per 1,000 live births)[a]	39.11
GDP per capita (purchasing power parity)[a]	$3,800
GDP real growth rate[a]	-1.7%
Human Development Index Level[b]	Medium
Human Development Index Rank (out of 182)[b]	114

Notes: [a]2009 estimates; [b]2008

Sources: CIA World Factbook, 2010
Human Development Report, 2009

Remittances and Migration by Continent

**Remittances Inflows to Guyana
by Continent of Origin**

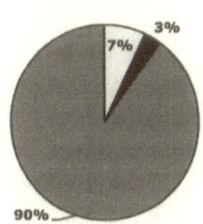

**Percent of Guyanese Migrants
by Continent of Destination**

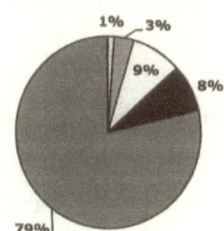

☐ Africa

▨ Asia

☐ Europe

■ Latin America &
Caribbean

▨ North America

▨ Oceania

Notes: Values are not displayed if they are less than 1 percent.
Source: Human Development Report, 2009

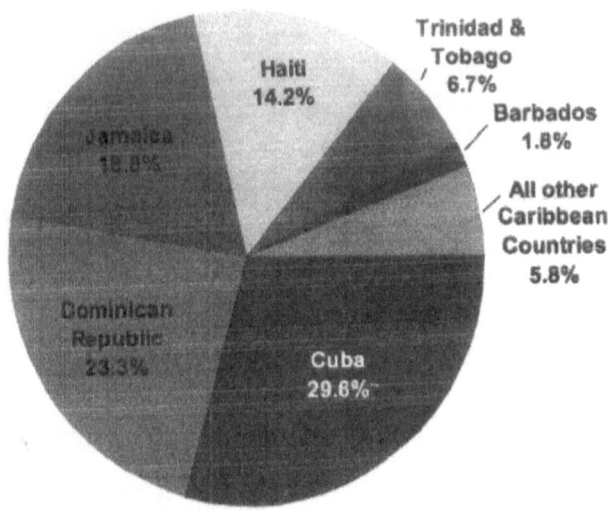

Total = 2,953,066

Note: Other Caribbean countries includes those reporting their birthplace as
Dominica, St. Lucia, St. Kitts-Nevis, Montserrat, Aruba, the Netherlands Antilles,
the Cayman Islands, the British Virgin Islands, Guadeloupe, Turks and Caicos
Islands, Martinique, Anguilla, the West Indies, and St. Barthelemy.
Source: US Census Bureau, Census 2000.

roreign Born by Region of Birth: 2002
(In percent)

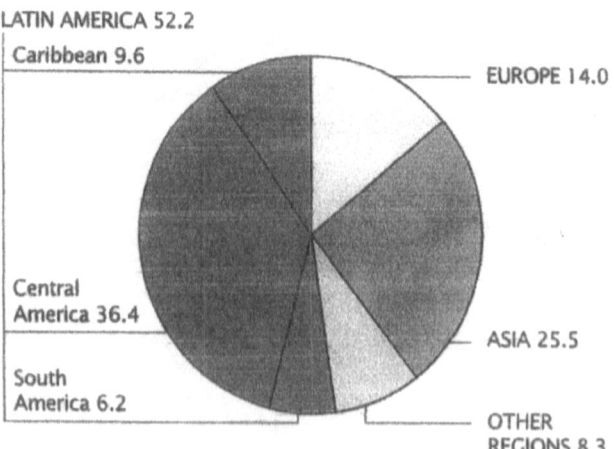

Source: U.S. Census Bureau, Current Population Survey, March 2002.

Jamaica

Key indicators, 2011

Population (millions)..2.8
GDP (US$ billions)..14.8
GDP per capita (US$).......................................5,402
GDP (PPP) as share (%) of world total...........0.03

GDP (PPP) per capita (int'l $), 1990–2011

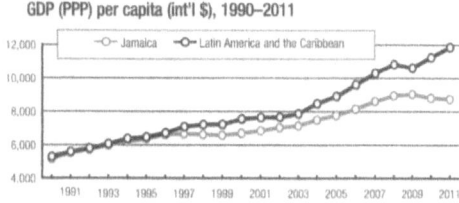

The Global Competitiveness Index

	Rank (out of 144)	Score (1–7)
GCI 2012–2013..	97	3.8
GCI 2011–2012 (out of 142)............................	107	3.8
GCI 2010–2011 (out of 139)............................	95	3.9
Basic requirements (40.0%)............................	114	3.8
Institutions..	87	3.6
Infrastructure..	85	3.6
Macroeconomic environment	141	2.9
Health and primary education......................	104	5.2
Efficiency enhancers (50.0%)........................	80	3.9
Higher education and training......................	75	4.1
Goods market efficiency	80	4.2
Labor market efficiency	77	4.3
Financial market development	55	4.3
Technological readiness...............................	73	3.8
Market size...	100	2.9
Innovation and sophistication factors (10.0%)...........	80	3.4
Business sophistication	79	3.8
Innovation..	86	3.0

Stage of development

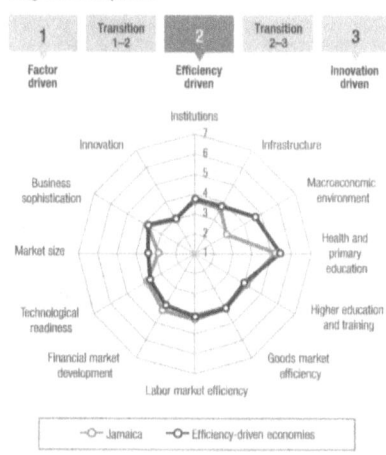

The most problematic factors for doing business

Crime and theft 17.7
Access to financing 14.8
Corruption 11.4
Tax rates...10.8
Inefficient government bureaucracy 9.8
Poor work ethic in national labor force 8.6
Tax regulations 6.6
Inflation..4.6
Inadequately educated workforce.....................4.3
Policy instability 3.1
Inadequate supply of infrastructure..................2.8
Government instability/coups 2.3
Insufficient capacity to innovate.......................2.2
Poor public health 0.5
Foreign currency regulations............................0.3
Restrictive labor regulations.............................0.3

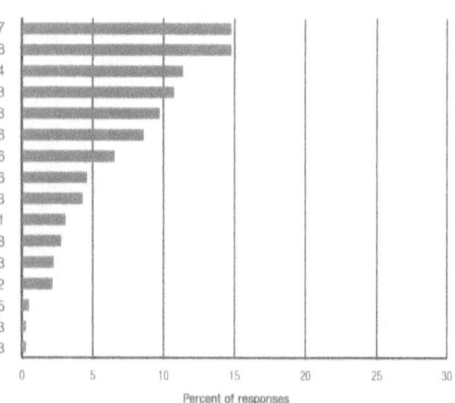

Barbados

Key indicators, 2011

Population (millions)	0.3
GDP (US$ billions)	4.5
GDP per capita (US$)	16,148
GDP (PPP) as share (%) of world total	0.01

GDP (PPP) per capita (int'l $), 1990–2011

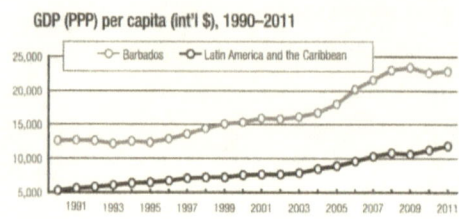

The Global Competitiveness Index

	Rank (out of 144)	Score (1–7)
GCI 2012–2013	44	4.4
GCI 2011–2012 (out of 142)	42	4.4
GCI 2010–2011 (out of 139)	43	4.5
Basic requirements (22.1%)	38	5.1
Institutions	24	5.1
Infrastructure	22	5.6
Macroeconomic environment	134	3.3
Health and primary education	16	6.4
Efficiency enhancers (50.0%)	49	4.4
Higher education and training	19	5.4
Goods market efficiency	64	4.3
Labor market efficiency	29	4.8
Financial market development	33	4.7
Technological readiness	30	5.1
Market size	134	2.0
Innovation and sophistication factors (27.9%)	38	4.0
Business sophistication	36	4.4
Innovation	40	3.6

Stage of development

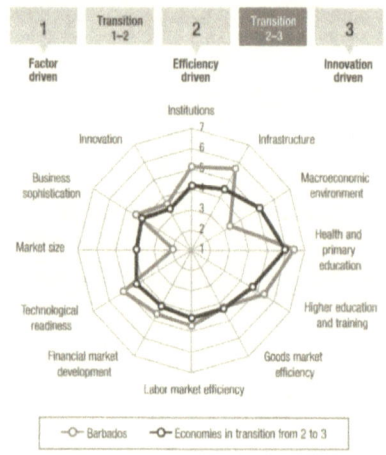

The most problematic factors for doing business

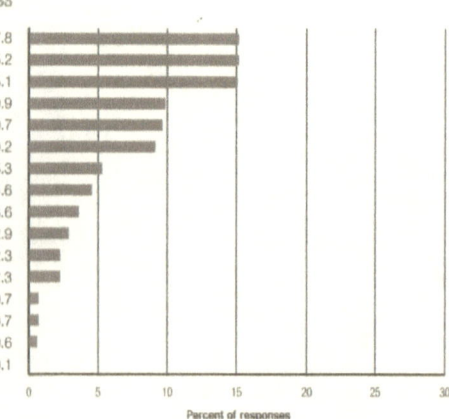

Inefficient government bureaucracy	17.8
Access to financing	15.2
Poor work ethic in national labor force	15.1
Insufficient capacity to innovate	9.9
Tax rates	9.7
Inflation	9.2
Restrictive labor regulations	5.3
Foreign currency regulations	4.6
Inadequate supply of infrastructure	3.6
Tax regulations	2.9
Crime and theft	2.3
Inadequately educated workforce	2.3
Government instability/coups	0.7
Policy instability	0.7
Corruption	0.6
Poor public health	0.1

Guyana

Key indicators, 2011

Population (millions)	0.8
GDP (US$ billions)	2.5
GDP per capita (US$)	3,202
GDP (PPP) as share (%) of world total	0.01

GDP (PPP) per capita (int'l $), 1990–2011

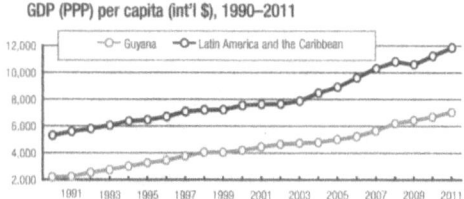

The Global Competitiveness Index

	Rank (out of 144)	Score (1–7)
GCI 2012–2013	109	3.7
GCI 2011–2012 (out of 142)	109	3.7
GCI 2010–2011 (out of 139)	110	3.6
Basic requirements (40.0%)	107	3.9
Institutions	100	3.5
Infrastructure	109	2.9
Macroeconomic environment	109	4.0
Health and primary education	99	5.3
Efficiency enhancers (50.0%)	109	3.6
Higher education and training	87	4.0
Goods market efficiency	84	4.2
Labor market efficiency	85	4.2
Financial market development	86	3.9
Technological readiness	94	3.4
Market size	132	2.0
Innovation and sophistication factors (10.0%)	71	3.5
Business sophistication	64	4.0
Innovation	76	3.1

Stage of development

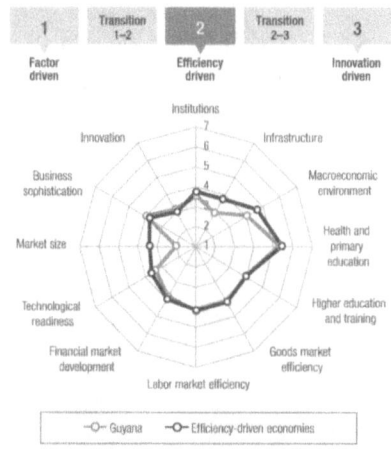

The most problematic factors for doing business

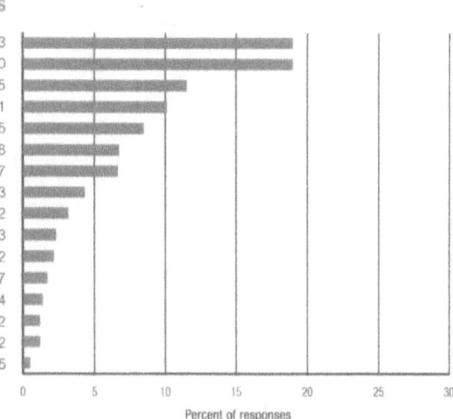

Crime and theft	19.3
Corruption	19.0
Tax rates	11.5
Access to financing	10.1
Poor work ethic in national labor force	8.5
Inadequately educated workforce	6.8
Inefficient government bureaucracy	6.7
Inadequate supply of infrastructure	4.3
Government instability/coups	3.2
Inflation	2.3
Poor public health	2.2
Insufficient capacity to innovate	1.7
Policy instability	1.4
Foreign currency regulations	1.2
Restrictive labor regulations	1.2
Tax regulations	0.5

Percent of responses

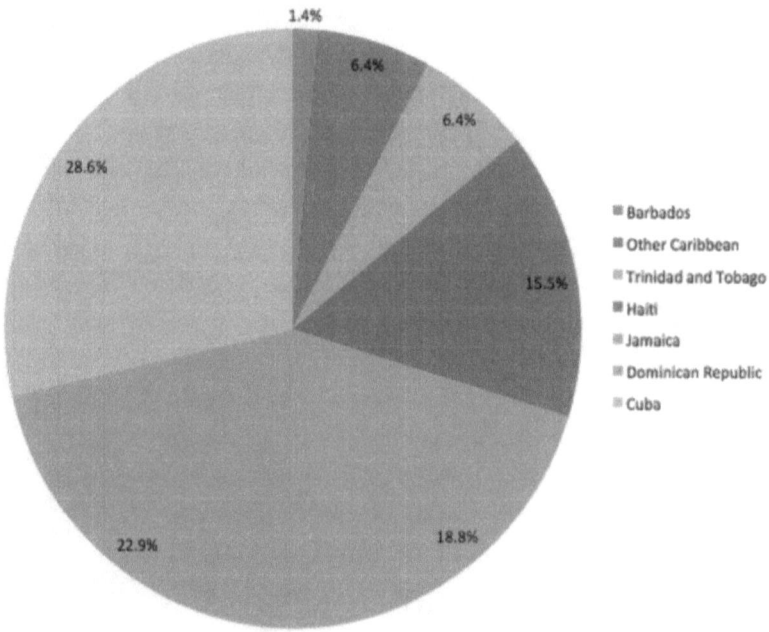

1.4%

6.4%

6.4%

28.6%

15.5%

■ Barbados
■ Other Caribbean
▦ Trinidad and Tobago
■ Haiti
▦ Jamaica
▦ Dominican Republic
▦ Cuba

22.9%

18.8%

Total = 3,465,890

Demographic and Social Characteristics

Trinidad and Tobago

Subject	Number	Percent	Subject	Number	Percent
Total population................................	197 400	100.0	**SEX AND AGE**		
U.S. CITIZENSHIP AND PERIOD OF U.S. ENTRY			Total population................................	197 400	100.0
Naturalized U.S. citizen................................	94 445	47.8	Male................................	85 420	43.3
Entered 1990 to 2000................................	13 685	6.9	Female................................	111 975	56.7
Entered 1980 to 1989................................	28 740	14.6			
Entered before 1980................................	52 025	26.4	Under 5 years................................	920	0.5
Not a U.S. citizen................................	102 950	52.2	5 to 9 years................................	2 640	1.3
Entered 1990 to 2000................................	54 365	27.5	10 to 14 years................................	7 455	3.8
Entered 1980 to 1989................................	31 690	16.1	15 to 19 years................................	13 120	6.6
Entered before 1980................................	16 895	8.6	20 to 24 years................................	13 955	7.1
			25 to 34 years................................	33 515	17.0
RACE			35 to 44 years................................	51 755	26.2
One race................................	166 465	84.3	45 to 54 years................................	36 870	18.7
White................................	6 870	3.5	55 to 59 years................................	12 980	6.6
Black or African American................................	135 510	68.6	60 to 64 years................................	9 180	4.7
American Indian and Alaska Native................................	1 095	0.6	65 to 74 years................................	10 065	5.1
Asian................................	17 820	9.0	75 to 84 years................................	3 880	2.0
Native Hawaiian and Other Pacific Islander................................	670	0.3	85 years and over................................	1 085	0.5
Some other race................................	4 500	2.3			
Two or more races................................	30 935	15.7	Median age (years)................................	40.1	(X)
HISPANIC OR LATINO ORIGIN			18 years and over................................	179 175	90.8
Hispanic or Latino (of any race)................................	3 735	1.9	Male................................	76 310	38.7
Not Hispanic or Latino................................	193 665	98.1	Female................................	102 865	52.1
White alone................................	6 240	3.2	21 years and over................................	170 115	86.2
			62 years and over................................	20 135	10.2
LANGUAGE SPOKEN AT HOME			65 years and over................................	15 005	7.6
Population 5 years and over................................	196 475	100.0	Male................................	5 570	2.8
English only................................	182 185	92.7	Female................................	9 440	4.8
Language other than English................................	14 295	7.3			
Speak English less than "very well"................................	3 570	1.8	**MARITAL STATUS**		
Spanish................................	7 345	3.7	Population 15 years and over................................	186 385	100.0
Speak English less than "very well"................................	1 775	0.9	Never married................................	55 640	29.9
Other Indo-European languages................................	5 645	2.9	Now married, excluding separated................................	92 550	49.7
Speak English less than "very well"................................	1 440	0.7	Separated................................	11 335	6.1
Asian and Pacific Island languages................................	755	0.4	Widowed................................	8 060	4.3
Speak English less than "very well"................................	265	0.1	Female................................	6 900	3.7
			Divorced................................	18 800	10.1
RELATIONSHIP			Female................................	12 360	6.6
Total population................................	197 400	100.0			
In households................................	194 420	98.5	**GRANDPARENTS AS CAREGIVERS**		
Householder................................	88 070	44.6	Grandparent living in household with one or		
Spouse................................	42 040	21.3	more own grandchildren under 18 years............	9 800	100.0
Child................................	33 300	16.9	Grandparent responsible for grandchildren................	3 585	36.6
Own child under 18 years................................	15 180	7.7			
Other relatives................................	19 500	9.9	**SCHOOL ENROLLMENT**		
Under 18 years................................	2 710	1.4	Population 3 years and over		
Nonrelatives................................	11 500	5.8	enrolled in school................................	41 435	100.0
Unmarried partner................................	4 690	2.4	Nursery school, preschool................................	265	0.6
In group quarters................................	2 980	1.5	Kindergarten................................	380	0.9
Institutionalized population................................	1 020	0.5	Elementary school (grades 1-8)................................	8 445	20.4
Noninstitutionalized population................................	1 960	1.0	High school (grades 9-12)................................	12 070	29.1
			College or graduate school................................	20 270	48.9
HOUSEHOLDS BY TYPE					
Total households³................................	88 075	100.0	**EDUCATIONAL ATTAINMENT**		
Family households (families)................................	65 250	74.1	Population 25 years and over................................	159 310	100.0
With own children under 18 years................................	36 960	42.0	Less than 9th grade................................	11 360	7.1
Married-couple family................................	38 095	43.3	9th to 12th grade, no diploma................................	23 910	15.0
With own children under 18 years................................	22 225	25.2	High school graduate (includes equivalency)................	48 000	30.1
Female householder, no husband present................................	22 120	25.1	Some college, no degree................................	33 015	20.7
With own children under 18 years................................	12 285	13.9	Associate degree................................	14 025	8.8
Nonfamily households................................	22 825	25.9	Bachelor's degree................................	18 840	11.8
Householder living alone................................	19 360	22.0	Graduate or professional degree................................	10 155	6.4
Householder 65 years and over................................	3 360	3.8			
			Percent high school graduate or higher................	(X)	77.9
RESIDENCE IN 1995			Percent bachelor's degree or higher................	(X)	18.2
Population 5 years and over................................	196 475	100.0			
Same house in 1995................................	95 425	48.6	**VETERAN STATUS**		
Different house in the U.S. in 1995................................	77 935	39.7	Civilian population 18 years and over............	178 060	100.0
Same county................................	47 750	24.3	Civilian veterans................................	7 935	4.5
Different county................................	30 185	15.4			
Same state................................	14 640	7.5			
Different state................................	15 545	7.9			
Elsewhere in 1995................................	23 120	11.8			

Source: US Census Bureau, Census 2000 Special Tabulations (STP-159)

Percentage of West Indian Children and Families Living below the Poverty Line

	Children	Families
West Indians in:		
New York State	17.9%	11.7%
The U.S.	19.5%	12.5%
Barbadians in:		
New York State	11.0%	6.6%
The U.S.	9.9%	6.5%
Belizeans in:		
New York State	5.9%	6.0%
The U.S.	24.8%	15.0%
British West Indians:		
New York State	11.8%	13.0%
The U.S.	22.5%	13.2%
Cubans in:		
New York State	21.9%	11.5%
The U.S.	17.0%	11.4%
Dutch West Indians in :		
New York State	10.9%	8.7%
The U.S.	22.0%	13.9%
Guyanese in:		
New York State	18.5%	11.9%
The U.S.	16.5%	10.7%
Haitians in:		
New York State	18.8%	14.6%
The U.S.	28.0%	20.7%
Jamaicans in:		
New York State	15.8%	10.6%
The U.S.	17.0%	11.1%
Trinidad and Tobagonians in:		
New York State	22.1%	13.1%
The U.S.	20.2%	12.7%

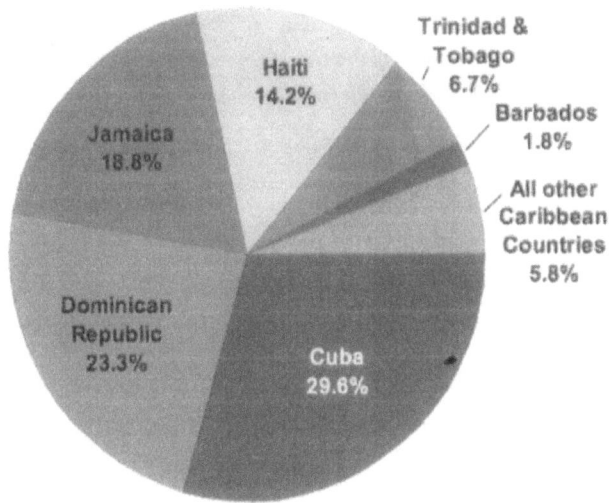

Total = 2,953,066

Note: Other Caribbean countries includes those reporting their birthplace as
Dominica, St. Lucia, St. Kitts-Nevis, Montserrat, Aruba, the Netherlands Antilles,
the Cayman Islands, the British Virgin Islands, Guadeloupe, Turks and Caicos
Islands, Martinique, Anguilla, the West Indies, and St. Barthelemy.
Source: US Census Bureau, Census 2000.

ᴦoreign Born by Region of Birth: 2002
(In percent)

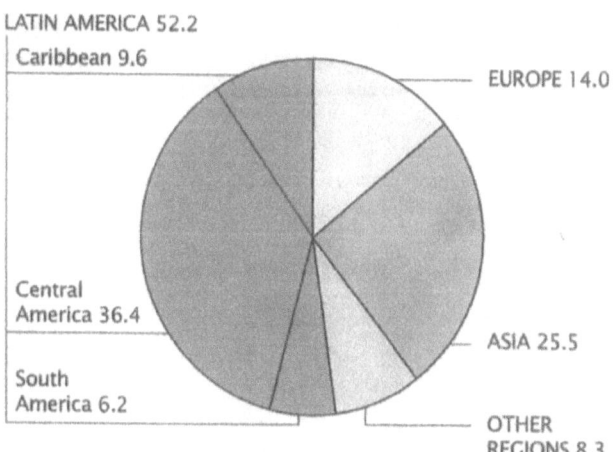

LATIN AMERICA 52.2

Caribbean 9.6

EUROPE 14.0

Central
America 36.4

ASIA 25.5

South
America 6.2

OTHER
REGIONS 8.3

Source: U.S. Census Bureau, Current Population Survey, March 2002.

- Median West Indian household income in 1989 was as follows:

Median West Indian Household Income in 1989

	New York State	United States
West Indian	$ 31,953	$ 28,083
Barbadian	$ 34,073	$ 33,928
Belizean	$ 33,600	$ 27,980
British West Indian	$ 29,756	$ 29,771
Cuban	$ 29,861	$ 28,056
Dutch West Indian	$ 36,559	$ 24,627
Guyanese	$ 33,390	$ 34,094
Haitian	$ 31,397	$ 36,053
Jamaican	$ 33,094	$ 27,754
Trinidad and Tobagonian	$ 30,348	$ 30,356

- West Indian median household income in 1989 was higher in New York State than elsewhere in the U.S.. In that state Dutch West Indian, Barbadian, Belizean and Guyanese (in that order) households earned the highest income while British West Indian and Cuban households earned the lowest. In the U.S. as a whole Haitian and Guyanese households earned the highest income in 1989 while Dutch West Indian households earned the lowest.

- Comparable median household income of *all* persons living in the U.S. mainland (in 1989) was :

Median Household Income

All persons in U.S.	$ 30,056
Black	$ 19,758
White	$ 31,435
Hispanic	$ 24,156
West Indian	**$ 28,083**

Participation Rates for the U.S. West Indian Population in 1990

	Male	Female	Total
West Indians in:			
New York State	80.2%	70.3%	75.2%
The U.S.	81.5%	63.6%	70.3%
Barbadians in:			
New York State	74.2%	71.9%	72.8%
The U.S.	77.9%	72.5%	74.2%
Belizeans in:			
New York State	82.9%	72.2%	77.5%
The U.S.	80.5%	70.0%	75.7%
British West Indians:			
New York State	80.7%	70.5%	74.7%
The U.S.	81.8%	72.2%	76.4%
Cubans in:			
New York State	\72.7%	55.6%	63.4%
The U.S.	75.4%	56.6%	65.3%
Dutch West Indians in :			
New York State	76.7%	67.8%	72.1%
The U.S.	72.3%	59.0%	67.6%
Guyanese in:			
New York State	79.1%	68.2%	73.5%
The U.S.	81.7%	69.4%	74.9%
Haitians in:			
New York State	81.0%	70.1%	75.2%
The U.S.	83.9%	70.9%	77.4%
Jamaicans in:			
New York State	76.8%	74.7%	75.2%
The U.S.	78.8%	75.2%	78.8%
Trinidad and Tobagonians in:			
New York State	77.5%	75.2%	77.4%
The U.S.	80.5%	75.0%	78.5%

- Unemployment appeared to be lowest among Dutch West Indians and Barbadians, and highest among Haitians. With the exception of Dutch West Indians , unemployment among West Indians in New York State was at least as great (and the vast majority of cases higher than) in the rest of the U.S.. Unemployment was distinctly higher among male than female West Indians. Participation rates tended to be lower among in New York Sate compared to the rest of the U.S., and distinctly higher among male compared with female West Indians. Participation Rates are

Caribbean Immigrants to the US over the Period 1990-1998

By Major Occupation

Countries	Professional Specialty or technical	Executive Administrative and Managerial	Sales	Administrative Support	Precision production Craft and repair	Operator fabricator and Labourer	Farming forestry and Fishing	Services	No Occupation	Total
Cuba	4874	1530	2801	3539	5908	27348	451	8818	74798	130067
Dominica Republic	12107	4695	5619	6615	14566	33748	14810	11594	204376	308130
Haiti	5237	1531	2424	2992	7653	13635	45935	8221	95035	182663
Jamaica	8109	2361	2335	7330	5433	8514	7181	29369	101152	171784
Trinidad & Tobago	3499	1254	870	2265	2285	2198	2224	5272	31842	51709
Other Caribbean	-	-	1047	2345	2558	2262	1450	9549	27772	46983
C'bn Total	33826	11371	15096	25086	38403	87705	72051	72823	534975	891336
G'bl Total	513749	236032	133030	208380	332563	707086	1241674	619780	4266355	8258649
C'bn Total as % of G'bl Total	6.58	5.35	11.35	12.04	11.55	12.40	5.80	11.75	12.54	89.36

Based on data from US Immigration and Naturalization Services, Statistical Yearbook of the Immigration and Naturalization Services, 1997 and 1998.

Net Remittance for Selected Caribbean Countries

(Percentage of GDP)

COUNTRY	1985	1986	1987	1988	1989	1990	1991	1992	1993	1994
Anguilla	NA	NA	NA	NA	NA	3.6	1	1.6	1.8	1.8
Antigua & Barbuda	NA	3.9	3.2	2.7	4.8	3.1	1.2	0.5	0.1	0.7
British Virgin Islands	NA	NA	NA	NA	-7.1	-8.3	-7.6	-7.4	-10	NA
Dominica	NA	1	6.1	6.2	6.6	6	5.9	5.7	6.1	4.6
Grenada	NA	6.2	8.7	9.2	8.7	7.7	7.6	7.3	6.7	8.8
Montserrat	NA	22.4	22.7	21.5	68.3	20.8	14	12.9	8.9	8.7
St. Kitts/Nevis	NA	8.3	8.7	8.9	10.7	6.8	6.8	6.5	5.7	6.8
St. Lucia	NA	5.4	7	3.7	3.4	2.8	3.7	2.4	0.9	2.6
St. Vincent/Grenadines	NA	7.7	6.1	5.3	5.8	6.2	4.9	4	3.8	5.6
The Bahamas	-0.8	-0.7	-0.8	-1.1	-0.6	-0.3	-0.3	-0.4	-0.4	NA
Barbados	1.6	1.8	1.8	2.2	2.1	2.3	2	2.6	1.6	NA
Belize	9.1	6.8	6.5	7.3	5.7	4.6	3.6	3.7	2.9	2.6
Guyana	2.4	1.9	3.2	3.1	3.7	3.3	3.6	3.7	3.3	NA
Jamaica	9.1	5.5	4.6	4.5	4	4.8	6.1	12.9	10.5	16.2
Suriname	-0.4	-0.2	0	-0.4	-0.4	-0.4	-0.4	-0.3	-0.1	NA
Trinidad & Tobago	-0.5	-0.6	-0.4	-0.5	-0.4	-0.4	-0.3	-0.3	-0.1	NA
The Dominican Republic	NA	4.4	6.9	6.5	4.5	5.5	4.2	3.9	3.8	NA
Haiti	2.4	2.3	2.8	3.2	2.8	2.6	2.6	2.6	2.3	1

Source: United Nations, Economic Commission for Latin America and the Caribbean, 1998 a

Skilled, Unskilled and Unemployed Migrants to the US,

Country	(1) Total immigrants in the US	(2) Total in US labour force	(3) % of (1) in US labour force	(4) Total not in US labour force	(5) % of (1) not in US labour force	(6) Total skilled of (2)	(7) % skilled of (2)	(8) Total non skilled of (2)	(9) % unskilled of (2)
Cuba	130067	55269	42.5	74798	57.5	12312	22.28	42957	77.72
Dominica Republic	308130	103754	33.7	204376	66.3	31368	30.23	72386	69.77
Haiti	182663	87628	47.9	95035	52.1	14421	16.46	73207	83.54
Jamaica	171784	70632	41.1	101152	58.9	15903	22.52	54729	77.48
Trinidad & Tobago	51709	19867	38.4	31842	61.6	7038	35.43	12829	64.57
Other Caribbean	46983	23498	50.0	27772	50.0	6845	29.13	16653	70.87
C'bn Total	891336	360648	40.5	534975	59.5	87887	24.37	272761	75.63
G'bl Total	8258649	3992294	48.3	4266355	51.7	1082344	27.11	2909950	72.89

Note: Changes have been made to the original titles of the columns by a consultant.
Based on data from US Immigration and Naturalization Services, Statistical Yearbook of the Immigration and Naturalization Services, 2000 and 2010

Educational Attainment for Adults (Ages 25 and Over) by Origin (%), 2005-09

	Educational Attainment				
	Less than High School	High School or GED	Some College	4-Year College (No Professional Degree)	Master's, Doctorate, or Professional Degree
US TOTAL	15	29	28	17	10
Native Born	12	31	30	18	10
Foreign Born	32	23	18	16	11
Black Immigrants	20	28	27	16	9
Black Immigrants Born in Africa	13	21	29	23	15
Black Immigrants Born in the Caribbean	22	32	27	13	7
Bahamas	12	26	32	19	10
St. Kitts-Nevis	19	32	21	18	10
Other Caribbean countries	19	30	24	15	12
Dominica	23	29	26	14	9
Other West Indian countries	16	35	26	15	8
Grenada	19	37	24	12	8
Jamaica	20	32	27	13	7
Trinidad and Tobago	14	36	29	14	7
Barbados	17	34	27	14	7
Antigua and Barbuda	20	32	25	15	7
Cuba	35	32	19	8	6
St. Vincent	20	35	25	14	6
Haiti	26	30	27	12	5
Dominican Republic	36	27	21	11	5
St. Lucia	21	39	22	12	5

Source: MPI analysis of 2005-09 ACS, pooled.

Caribbean Blacks are more likely to be English-proficient than their African counterparts (see Table 5). A smaller proportion of the former are also likely to be bilingual; in fact, close to 60 percent of Black Caribbean immigrants speak exclusively English at home. These patterns reflect the fact that the majority of Caribbean countries are former British colonies. As the estimates indicate, 90 percent of immigrants from major English-speaking Caribbean-origin countries — such as Jamaica, Trinidad and Tobago, and Barbados — use English as their primary language at home. Moreover, 11 of 13 Caribbean-origin groups in Table 4 have English monolingual levels that exceed the average for all immigrants and that for Black Africans.

Black Caribbean Immigrants by Country of Origin, United States, 1980 to 2008-09

	Population (thousands)				Share of Total from Region (%)				
Year	1980	2000	2006	2008-09	1980	1990	2000	2006	2008-09
Black Caribbean Immigrants	453	1,428	1,636	1,701	100	100	100	100	100
Jamaica	179	534	620	612	40	35	37	38	36
Haiti	87	414	484	534	19	24	29	30	31
Trinidad & Tobago	57	164	194	181	13	11	11	12	11
Dominican Republic	14	85	68	110	3	11	6	4	6
Barbados	27	51	51	48	6	4	4	3	3
Cuba	12	30	33	34	3	2	2	2	2
Grenada	7	26	30	29	2	2	2	2	2
Other West Indian countries	3	25	39	29	1	2	2	2	2
Bahamas	12	25	26	26	3	2	2	2	2
St. Lucia	1	13	17	18	0	1	1	1	1
Antigua-Barbuda	4	18	14	17	1	1	1	1	1
St. Vincent	3	21	20	17	1	1	1	1	1
Dominica	1	13	15	16	0	1	1	1	1
Other Caribbean countries	43	-	15	16	9	2	-	1	1
St. Kitts-Nevis	2	10	9	12	0	1	1	1	1

Note: Black immigrants are those who responded "Black" either alone or in combination with any other race to the ACS race question in 2000, 2006, 2008, and 2009. In 1980 and 1990, respondents could not report more than one race (i.e., report a multiracial identity), and so the responses for these years are for Black race only.
Source: MPI analysis of data from the 1980, 1990, and 2000 US Census of Population and Housing; 2006 ACS, and 2008-2009 ACS, pooled.

Percent Distribution of the Foreign Born From Latin America and the Caribbean by Region of Birth and State: 2010

(Numbers in thousands. Data based on sample. For information on confidentiality protection, sampling error, nonsampling error, and definitions, see www.census.gov/acs/www)

Area	Latin America		Caribbean		Central America						South America	
					Total		Mexico		Other Central America¹			
	Number	Margin of error (±)²	Percent of total	Margin of error (±)³	Percent of total	Margin of error (±)²	Percent of total	Margin of error (±)²	Percent of total	Margin of error (±)²	Percent of total	Margin of error (±)²
United States...	21,224	90	17.6	0.2	69.6	0.2	55.2	0.3	14.4	0.2	12.9	0.2
Alabama	98	5	5.4	1.6	86.8	2.6	70.0	3.8	16.7	3.5	7.8	2.1
Alaska	9	2	16.4	9.3	68.0	9.0	56.2	11.5	11.8	8.2	15.6	6.2
Arizona	572	13	2.2	0.5	94.9	0.7	90.4	1.0	4.5	0.9	2.9	0.5
Arkansas	88	5	1.7	0.9	94.4	1.6	73.4	3.6	21.0	3.6	3.9	1.5
California	5,477	43	1.3	0.1	94.4	0.2	78.8	0.5	15.6	0.4	4.4	0.2
Colorado	275	11	2.4	0.6	93.1	1.0	84.5	1.7	8.6	1.4	4.5	0.9
Connecticut	205	11	36.3	2.6	26.2	3.0	10.2	1.9	16.0	2.7	37.5	3.2
Delaware	34	3	16.5	4.1	65.9	6.3	49.7	7.9	16.2	5.6	17.6	5.4
District of Columbia....	36	3	20.8	4.8	59.8	6.7	10.8	5.1	49.0	7.5	19.4	5.1
Florida	2,752	30	55.1	0.9	21.5	0.8	9.6	0.5	11.9	0.6	23.4	0.7
Georgia	515	12	16.4	1.3	72.5	1.5	56.3	2.0	16.2	1.6	11.1	1.0
Hawaii	13	3	14.7	7.9	55.6	9.0	41.0	9.1	14.6	5.8	29.7	7.9
Idaho	54	4	1.2	0.9	93.4	2.0	88.2	3.1	5.2	3.1	5.4	1.8
Illinois	842	16	3.0	0.4	90.2	0.9	84.1	1.1	6.1	0.8	6.8	0.8
Indiana	143	6	4.9	1.1	89.2	1.8	76.9	2.6	12.3	2.1	5.9	1.4
Iowa	60	4	2.1	1.2	91.0	2.6	75.0	4.4	16.0	3.8	6.9	2.5
Kansas	106	6	1.0	0.5	94.0	1.5	83.8	2.5	10.2	2.5	5.0	1.4
Kentucky	60	4	16.3	3.3	76.0	3.9	60.7	4.8	15.3	3.7	7.8	2.1
Louisiana	93	5	11.3	2.4	79.2	2.8	32.6	3.5	46.6	3.6	9.5	2.4
Maine	4	1	34.5	12.6	25.2	14.0	11.8	10.9	13.4	8.8	40.4	14.2
Maryland	312	9	16.9	1.6	63.0	1.9	11.3	1.5	51.7	2.5	20.1	1.7
Massachusetts	356	13	42.6	2.1	24.0	1.9	4.4	0.9	19.6	1.9	33.4	2.1
Michigan	118	7	11.9	2.2	78.3	2.9	67.7	3.5	10.6	2.1	9.8	1.7
Minnesota	104	5	4.7	1.4	77.5	3.1	63.4	3.7	14.1	2.7	17.8	2.8
Mississippi	32	3	8.9	4.4	78.5	5.5	64.3	6.5	14.3	5.1	12.5	4.9
Missouri	72	6	11.9	3.0	77.2	3.6	62.5	4.2	14.7	3.2	10.9	2.5
Montana	2	1	6.7	6.7	45.0	16.2	41.5	17.3	3.6	4.5	48.3	16.1
Nebraska	61	4	1.9	1.1	94.2	1.8	75.0	4.8	19.3	4.7	3.9	1.6
Nevada	291	8	6.7	1.0	88.4	1.4	75.1	1.8	13.3	1.7	5.0	0.9
New Hampshire	14	3	31.4	9.9	35.2	11.0	20.8	11.0	14.4	6.0	33.5	10.8
New Jersey	852	15	32.4	1.5	30.9	1.3	15.2	1.1	15.6	1.1	36.8	1.5
New Mexico	163	9	2.2	0.7	95.1	1.4	91.4	1.6	3.7	1.3	2.7	1.0
New York	2,155	28	49.3	0.9	23.9	0.9	11.7	0.8	12.1	0.7	26.8	0.8
North Carolina	414	11	7.1	1.2	83.2	1.5	63.5	2.3	19.7	1.8	9.7	1.1
North Dakota	1	1	25.4	17.6	63.7	18.4	50.7	18.5	13.0	13.9	10.9	8.9
Ohio	101	6	13.7	3.6	70.3	4.3	53.8	4.8	16.5	3.0	16.0	3.1
Oklahoma	121	6	1.6	0.9	93.4	1.7	83.3	2.8	10.1	2.4	5.0	1.5
Oregon	175	8	2.2	0.8	94.0	1.1	86.2	2.0	7.9	2.0	3.7	0.8
Pennsylvania	221	11	39.6	2.8	38.2	2.7	26.7	2.3	11.5	1.7	22.2	2.3
Rhode Island	60	4	45.4	5.3	36.1	4.9	6.9	2.5	29.2	4.8	18.5	4.7
South Carolina	120	6	7.6	1.8	81.6	2.8	57.8	4.0	23.8	3.8	10.7	2.1
South Dakota	6	1	1.5	1.9	87.0	6.2	64.1	15.4	22.9	14.8	11.5	6.0
Tennessee	143	7	5.3	1.4	87.4	2.4	63.3	4.7	24.1	3.8	7.3	1.7
Texas	3,013	35	2.0	0.2	94.0	0.3	82.5	0.5	11.5	0.5	4.0	0.3
Utah	139	6	1.6	0.9	82.5	2.4	73.8	2.7	8.8	1.7	15.9	2.3
Vermont	3	1	18.0	11.9	40.1	20.5	33.7	22.0	6.5	5.7	41.9	15.7
Virginia	338	9	8.5	1.1	63.7	2.1	19.1	2.3	44.6	2.6	27.8	2.1
Washington	277	8	2.0	0.5	91.5	1.1	84.2	1.6	7.4	1.1	6.4	1.0
West Virginia	5	1	21.5	9.7	57.7	11.7	22.9	8.9	34.8	13.0	20.8	10.0
Wisconsin	110	6	3.7	1.0	88.1	2.3	80.3	2.5	7.7	1.8	8.2	2.0
Wyoming	9	2	–	–	84.4	9.5	75.1	10.3	9.3	6.7	15.6	9.5

– Represents or rounds to zero.

¹ Other Central America includes Belize, Costa Rica, El Salvador, Guatemala, Honduras, Nicaragua, and Panama.

² Data are based on a sample and are subject to sampling variability. A margin of error is a measure of an estimate's variability. The larger the margin of error is in relation to the size of the estimate, the less reliable the estimate. This number when added to and subtracted from the estimate forms the 90 percent confidence interval.

Source: U.S. Census Bureau, 2010 American Community Survey.

Trinidad and Tobago

Key indicators, 2011

Population (millions)..1.4
GDP (US$ billions)..22.7
GDP per capita (US$)...................................17,158
GDP (PPP) as share (%) of world total............0.03

GDP (PPP) per capita (int'l $), 1990–2011

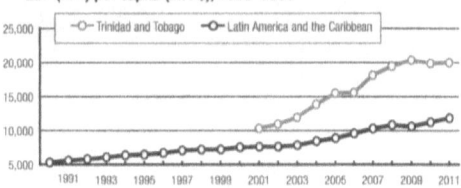

The Global Competitiveness Index

	Rank (out of 144)	Score (1–7)
GCI 2012–2013	84	4.0
GCI 2011–2012 (out of 142)	81	4.0
GCI 2010–2011 (out of 139)	84	4.0
Basic requirements (25.8%)	41	4.9
Institutions	91	3.6
Infrastructure	55	4.3
Macroeconomic environment	19	6.0
Health and primary education	55	5.8
Efficiency enhancers (50.0%)	83	3.9
Higher education and training	71	4.2
Goods market efficiency	106	3.9
Labor market efficiency	110	4.0
Financial market development	60	4.2
Technological readiness	60	4.1
Market size	107	2.8
Innovation and sophistication factors (24.2%)	89	3.3
Business sophistication	84	3.8
Innovation	104	2.9

Stage of development

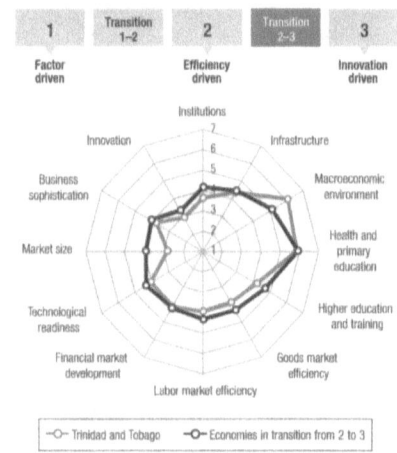

The most problematic factors for doing business

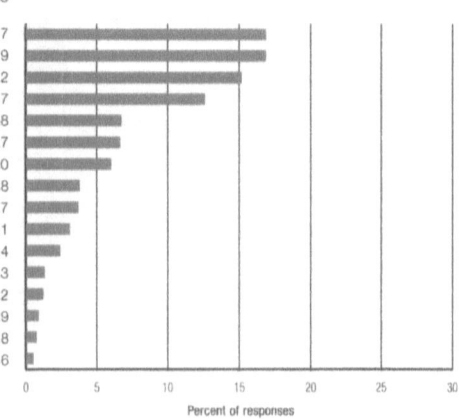

Inefficient government bureaucracy 17.7
Crime and theft 16.9
Poor work ethic in national labor force 15.2
Corruption 12.7
Access to financing 6.8
Inadequate supply of infrastructure....................................6.7
Insufficient capacity to innovate 6.0
Policy instability 3.8
Inadequately educated workforce.......................................3.7
Restrictive labor regulations..3.1
Inflation..2.4
Tax rates...1.3
Foreign currency regulations...1.2
Poor public health 0.9
Government instability/coups 0.8
Tax regulations 0.6

English Proficiency for Immigrants Ages 5 and Over by Origin (%), 2005-09

	Speaks Another Language at Home				
	Yes, Speaks Only English	Yes, Speaks English Very Well	Yes Speaks English Well	Yes, Speaks English but Not Well	Does Not Speak English
Foreign Born, Total	16	32	21	20	11
Black Immigrants, Total	46	29	14	8	3
Black African Immigrants	21	49	20	8	2
Black Caribbean Immigrants	59	19	12	8	3
Grenada	97	2	0	0	0
Barbados	96	3	0	1	0
St. Vincent	96	3	1	0	0
Antigua-Barbuda	96	3	0	0	0
Trinidad	95	3	1	0	0
St. Kitts-Nevis	95	4	0	0	0
Jamaica	93	6	1	0	0
Other West Indian countries	88	9	2	1	0
Bahamas	77	20	3	1	0
Other Caribbean countries	72	22	5	1	0
Dominica	62	26	6	3	3
St. Lucia	59	34	5	2	0
Cuba	8	26	20	26	20
Haiti	7	40	30	18	5
Dominican Republic	5	31	24	26	14

Source: MPI analysis of 2005-2009 ACS, pooled.

Black Immigrants as Share of All Immigrants in the United States from Caribbean Origins, 2008-09

	Total Immigrants (thousands)	Black Immigrants (thousands)	% Black
All US Immigrants	*38,234*	*3,267*	*9%*
Born in the Caribbean	3,437	1,701	49%
St. Kitts-Nevis	12	12	100%
Haiti	541	534	99%
Barbados	50	48	96%
Jamaica	638	612	96%
St. Lucia	19	18	95%
Antigua-Barbuda	18	17	94%
St. Vincent	18	17	94%
Grenada	31	29	94%
Bahamas	29	26	90%
Other West Indian countries	34	29	85%
Trinidad and Tobago	220	181	82%
Other Caribbean countries	23	16	70%
Dominica	34	16	47%
Dominican Republic	785	110	14%
Cuba	985	34	3%

Source: MPI analysis of 2008 and 2009 ACS, pooled.

Haiti

Key indicators, 2011

Population (millions) 10.2
GDP (US$ billions) 7.4
GDP per capita (US$) 738
GDP (PPP) as share (%) of world total 0.02

GDP (PPP) per capita (int'l $), 1990–2011

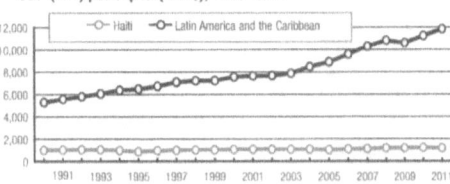

The Global Competitiveness Index

	Rank (out of 144)	Score (1–7)
GCI 2012–2013	142	2.9
GCI 2011–2012 (out of 142)	141	2.9
GCI 2010–2011 (out of 139)	n/a	n/a
Basic requirements (60.0%)	140	3.0
Institutions	143	2.5
Infrastructure	144	1.5
Macroeconomic environment	86	4.4
Health and primary education	134	3.6
Efficiency enhancers (35.0%)	143	2.8
Higher education and training	144	1.9
Goods market efficiency	142	3.0
Labor market efficiency	83	4.2
Financial market development	141	2.6
Technological readiness	138	2.5
Market size	127	2.3
Innovation and sophistication factors (5.0%)	143	2.4
Business sophistication	142	2.8
Innovation	143	2.0

Stage of development

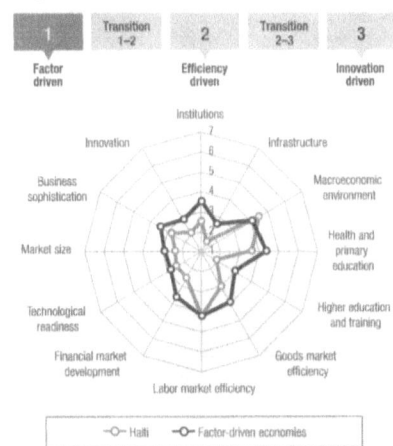

The most problematic factors for doing business

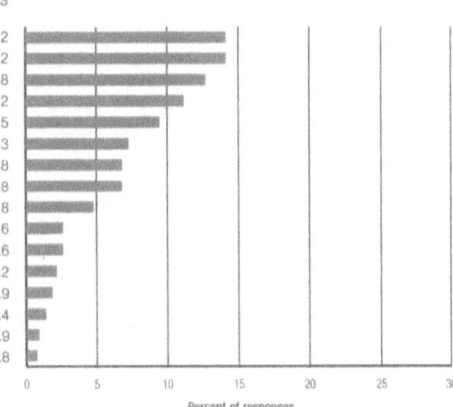

Access to financing 14.2
Corruption 14.2
Policy instability 12.8
Inadequate supply of infrastructure 11.2
Government instability/coups 9.5
Crime and theft 7.3
Inadequately educated workforce 6.8
Inefficient government bureaucracy 6.8
Poor work ethic in national labor force 4.8
Restrictive labor regulations 2.6
Tax regulations 2.6
Tax rates 2.2
Poor public health 1.9
Foreign currency regulations 1.4
Inflation 0.9
Insufficient capacity to innovate 0.8

Remittances Profile: Guyana

Formal Remittances Inflows

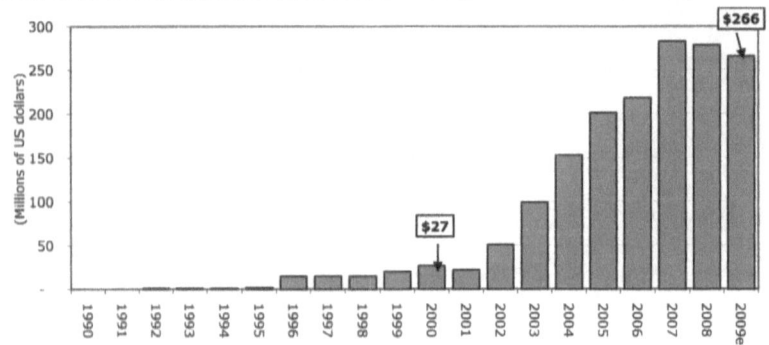

Source: Remittances data, Development Prospects Group, World Bank, 2010

Remittances Inflows as a Share of Selected Financial Flows and GDP, 2008
Remittances flows constitute an important source of foreign exchange for developing economies. Comparing remittances to other financial inflows displays the extent to which remittances contribute to a country's inflow of foreign exchange.

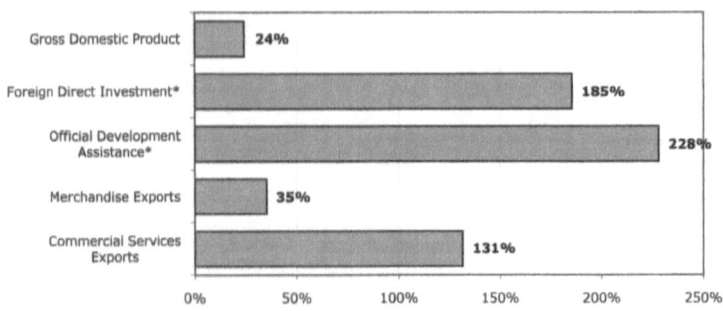

*FDI and ODA rates are based on 2007 data

Sources: International Trade Statistics, World Trade Organization, 2009
Remittances data, Development Prospects Group, World Bank, 2009
World Development Indicators, World Bank, 2010

Census 2000- Demographic Profile

Trinidad and Tobago

Subject	Number	Percent	Subject	Number	Percent
EMPLOYMENT STATUS			COMMUTING TO WORK		
Population 16 years and over	184 105	100.0	Workers 16 years and over	114 650	100.0
In labor force	127 795	69.4	Car, truck, or van - - drove alone	55 770	48.6
Civilian labor force	126 680	68.8	Car, truck, or van - - carpooled	13 845	12.1
Employed	117 300	63.7	Public transportation (including taxicab)	36 735	32.0
Unemployed	9 380	5.1	Walked	4 780	4.2
Percent of civilian labor force	(X)	7.4	Other means	1 090	1.0
Armed Forces	1 115	0.6	Worked at home	2 430	2.1
Not in labor force	56 305	30.6	Mean travel time to work (minutes)	39.7	(X)
Females 16 years and over	105 295	100.0	INCOME IN 1999		
In labor force	69 015	65.5	Households[2]	88 075	100.0
Civilian labor force	68 755	65.3	Less than $10,000	9 675	11.0
Employed	63 640	60.4	$10,000 to $14,999	4 735	5.4
			$15,000 to $24,999	11 240	12.8
Own children under 6 years	1 055	100.0	$25,000 to $34,999	12 815	14.6
All parents in family in labor force	555	52.6	$35,000 to $49,999	14 360	16.3
			$50,000 to $74,999	17 460	19.8
Employed civilian population			$75,000 to $99,999	8 925	10.1
16 years and over	117 300	100.0	$100,000 to $149,999	6 435	7.3
OCCUPATION			$150,000 to $199,999	1 285	1.5
Management, professional, and related occupations	34 820	29.7	$200,000 or more	1 150	1.3
Service occupations	26 925	23.0	Median household income (dollars)	40 168	(X)
Sales and office occupations	31 945	27.2			
Farming, fishing, and forestry occupations	90	0.1	With earnings	79 150	89.9
Construction, extraction, and maintenance			Mean earnings (dollars)	51 670	(X)
occupations	11 075	9.4	With Social Security income	10 930	12.4
Production, transportation, and material moving			Mean Social Security income (dollars)	8 830	(X)
occupations	12 445	10.6	With Supplemental Security income	3 575	4.1
			Mean Supplemental Security income (dollars)	6 024	(X)
INDUSTRY			With public assistance income	3 590	4.1
Agriculture, forestry, fishing and hunting, and mining	185	0.2	Mean public assistance income (dollars)	3 356	(X)
Construction	6 655	5.7	With retirement income	7 600	8.6
Manufacturing	7 955	6.8	Mean retirement income (dollars)	15 562	(X)
Wholesale trade	2 720	2.3			
Retail trade	11 235	9.6	Families[2]	65 250	100.0
Transportation and warehousing, and utilities	8 770	7.5	Less than $10,000	5 455	8.4
Information	3 575	3.0	$10,000 to $14,999	2 920	4.5
Finance, insurance, real estate, and rental and			$15,000 to $24,999	7 660	11.7
leasing	10 900	9.3	$25,000 to $34,999	8 915	13.7
Professional, scientific, management, administrative,			$35,000 to $49,999	10 885	16.7
and waste management services	10 810	9.2	$50,000 to $74,999	14 475	22.2
Educational, health and social services	35 070	29.9	$75,000 to $99,999	7 695	11.8
Arts, entertainment, recreation, accommodation and			$100,000 to $149,999	5 465	8.4
food services	6 120	5.2	$150,000 to $199,999	1 040	1.6
Other services (except public administration)	8 215	7.0	$200,000 or more	840	1.3
Public administration	5 085	4.3	Median family income (dollars)	45 240	(X)
CLASS OF WORKER			Per capita income (dollars)	23 026	(X)
Private wage and salary workers	92 745	79.1	Median earnings (dollars):		
Government workers	18 765	16.0	Male full-time, year-round workers	33 009	(X)
Self-employed workers in own not incorporated			Female full-time, year-round workers	28 933	(X)

Subject	Number	Percent	Subject	Number below poverty level	Percent below poverty level
business	5 555	4.7			
Unpaid family workers	235	0.2			
			POVERTY STATUS IN 1999		
DISABILITY STATUS OF THE CIVILIAN			Families[3]	8 085	12.4
NONINSTITUTIONALIZED POPULATION			With related children under 18 years	6 270	15.0
Population 5 to 20 years	26 135	100.0	With related children under 5 years	2 615	17.2
With a disability	2 695	10.3	Families with female householder, no		
Population 21 to 64 years	153 415	100.0	husband present[3]	4 675	22.0
With a disability	36 080	23.5	With related children under 18 years	4 085	27.0
Percent employed	(X)	67.2	With related children under 5 years	1 650	33.9
No disability	117 335	76.5	Individuals	26 670	13.7
Percent employed	(X)	73.2	18 years and over	22 800	12.9
Population 65 years and over	14 790	100.0	65 years and over	2 355	15.9
With a disability	5 795	39.2	Related children under 18 years	3 670	20.5
			Related children 5 to 17 years	3 380	19.9
			Unrelated individuals 15 years and over	8 550	24.8

Source: US Census Bureau, Census 2000 Special Tabulations (STP-159)

Percent of the Foreign Born From Latin America and the Caribbean Who Are Naturalized U.S. Citizens by Place of Birth: 2010

(Data based on sample. For information on confidentiality protection, sampling error, nonsampling error, and definitions, see *www.census.gov/acs/www*)

Region and country of birth	Percent	
	Estimate	Margin of error (±)[1]
Total	32.1	0.3
Caribbean	54.1	0.6
Cuba	55.7	1.2
Dominican Republic............	47.7	1.4
Haiti........................	50.0	1.6
Jamaica	61.2	1.5
Other Caribbean [2]	57.7	1.6
Central America.................	24.3	0.3
Mexico......................	22.9	0.3
El Salvador..................	27.9	1.0
Guatemala....................	24.1	1.3
Honduras....................	21.1	1.4
Other Central America [3].........	52.1	1.5
South America..................	44.4	0.6
Brazil	28.2	1.7
Colombia	48.2	1.3
Ecuador.....................	40.7	1.8
Peru........................	43.2	1.7
Other South America [4]..........	50.3	1.1

[1] Data are based on a sample and are subject to sampling variability. A margin of error is a measure of an estimate's variability. The larger the margin of error is in relation to the size of the estimate, the less reliable the estimate. This number when added to and subtracted from the estimate forms the 90 percent confidence interval.

[2] Other Caribbean includes Anguilla, Antigua and Barbuda, Aruba, Bahamas, Barbados, British Virgin Islands, Cayman Islands, Dominica, Grenada, the former country of Guadeloupe (including St. Barthélemy and Saint-Martin), Martinique, Montserrat, the former country of the Netherlands Antilles (including Bonaire, Curaçao, Saba, Sint Eustatius, and Sint Maarten), St. Kitts and Nevis, St. Lucia, St. Vincent and the Grenadines, Trinidad and Tobago, and Turks and Caicos Islands.

[3] Other Central America includes Belize, Costa Rica, Nicaragua, and Panama.

[4] Other South America includes Argentina, Bolivia, Chile, Falkland Islands, French Guiana, Guyana, Paraguay, Suriname, Uruguay, and Venezuela.

Source: U.S. Census Bureau, 2010 American Community Survey.

Census 2000- Demographic Profile

Barbados

Subject	Number	Percent
EMPLOYMENT STATUS		
Population 16 years and over	50 410	100.0
In labor force	34 415	68.3
Civilian labor force	34 000	67.4
Employed	31 815	63.1
Unemployed	2 185	4.3
Percent of civilian labor force	(X)	6.4
Armed Forces	415	0.8
Not in labor force	15 995	31.7
Females 16 years and over	28 330	100.0
In labor force	18 630	65.8
Civilian labor force	18 510	65.3
Employed	17 270	61.0
Own children under 6 years	240	100.0
All parents in family in labor force	165	68.8
Employed civilian population 16 years and over	31 815	100.0
OCCUPATION		
Management, professional, and related occupations	9 340	29.4
Service occupations	8 165	25.7
Sales and office occupations	8 470	26.6
Farming, fishing, and forestry occupations	30	0.1
Construction, extraction, and maintenance occupations	2 640	8.3
Production, transportation, and material moving occupations	3 165	9.9
INDUSTRY		
Agriculture, forestry, fishing and hunting, and mining	65	0.2
Construction	1 340	4.2
Manufacturing	1 745	5.5
Wholesale trade	575	1.8
Retail trade	2 405	7.6
Transportation and warehousing, and utilities	2 535	8.0
Information	995	3.1
Finance, insurance, real estate, and rental and leasing	3 255	10.2
Professional, scientific, management, administrative, and waste management services	2 550	8.0
Educational, health and social services	10 480	32.9
Arts, entertainment, recreation, accommodation and food services	2 000	6.3
Other services (except public administration)	2 250	7.1
Public administration	1 625	5.1
CLASS OF WORKER		
Private wage and salary workers	24 420	76.8
Government workers	6 245	19.6
Self-employed workers in own not incorporated business	1 105	3.5
Unpaid family workers	50	0.2
DISABILITY STATUS OF THE CIVILIAN NONINSTITUTIONALIZED POPULATION		
Population 5 to 20 years	3 190	100.0
With a disability	335	10.5
Population 21 to 64 years	40 795	100.0
With a disability	10 255	25.1
Percent employed	(X)	67.4
No disability	30 540	74.9
Percent employed	(X)	75.5
Population 65 years and over	7 365	100.0
With a disability	3 110	42.2

Subject	Number	Percent
COMMUTING TO WORK		
Workers 16 years and over	31 290	100.0
Car, truck, or van - - drove alone	14 440	46.1
Car, truck, or van - - carpooled	3 455	11.0
Public transportation (including taxicab)	11 510	36.8
Walked	1 125	3.6
Other means	280	0.9
Worked at home	480	1.5
Mean travel time to work (minutes)	41.3	(X)
INCOME IN 1999		
Households[2]	26 680	100.0
Less than $10,000	3 080	11.5
$10,000 to $14,999	1 455	5.5
$15,000 to $24,999	3 605	13.5
$25,000 to $34,999	3 595	13.5
$35,000 to $49,999	4 055	15.2
$50,000 to $74,999	5 445	20.4
$75,000 to $99,999	2 670	10.0
$100,000 to $149,999	1 870	7.0
$150,000 to $199,999	455	1.7
$200,000 or more	450	1.7
Median household income (dollars)	40 452	(X)
With earnings	22 915	85.9
Mean earnings (dollars)	53 251	(X)
With Social Security income	5 095	19.1
Mean Social Security income (dollars)	9 793	(X)
With Supplemental Security Income	1 360	5.1
Mean Supplemental Security Income (dollars)	6 479	(X)
With public assistance income	1 110	4.2
Mean public assistance income (dollars)	3 939	(X)
With retirement income	3 250	12.2
Mean retirement income (dollars)	17 452	(X)
Families[2]	18 625	100.0
Less than $10,000	1 325	7.1
$10,000 to $14,999	715	3.8
$15,000 to $24,999	2 105	11.3
$25,000 to $34,999	2 405	12.9
$35,000 to $49,999	3 010	16.2
$50,000 to $74,999	4 390	23.6
$75,000 to $99,999	2 340	12.6
$100,000 to $149,999	1 620	8.7
$150,000 to $199,999	400	2.1
$200,000 or more	315	1.7
Median family income (dollars)	48 460	(X)
Per capita income (dollars)	26 052	(X)
Median earnings (dollars):		
Male full-time, year-round workers	35 357	(X)
Female full-time, year-round workers	29 713	(X)

Subject	Number below poverty level	Percent below poverty level
POVERTY STATUS IN 1999		
Families[3]	1 865	10.0
With related children under 18 years	1 450	13.6
With related children under 5 years	610	16.7
Families with female householder, no husband present[3]	1 185	17.8
With related children under 18 years	1 000	24.0
With related children under 5 years	390	28.7
Individuals	6 240	12.1
18 years and over	5 690	11.6
65 years and over	1 175	16.0
Related children under 18 years	515	22.1
Related children 5 to 17 years	495	23.2
Unrelated individuals 15 years and over	2 835	23.8

Source: US Census Bureau, Census 2000 Special Tabulations (STP-159)

International Migration

Total immigrants[a]	11,599
Total refugees[a]	..
Total emigrants[b]	417,469
Skilled emigration rate, tertiary educated[c]	85.9%
Average annual net migration[d]	-8,000

Notes: [a]2010; [b]2005; [c]2000; [d]2005-2010
Sources: International Migrant Stock, 2009
World Population Prospects, 2008
Migration and Remittances Factbook, 2008

Selected Socioeconomic Indicators

Total population[a]	752,940
Annual population growth[a]	-0.63%
Life expectancy at birth[b]	66.31
Infant mortality rate (per 1,000 live births)[a]	39.11
GDP per capita (purchasing power parity)[a]	$3,800
GDP real growth rate[a]	-1.7%
Human Development Index Level[b]	Medium
Human Development Index Rank (out of 182)[b]	114

Notes: [a]2009 estimates; [b]2008
Sources: CIA World Factbook, 2010
Human Development Report, 2009

Remittances and Migration by Continent

Remittances Inflows to Guyana by Continent of Origin

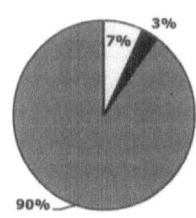

Percent of Guyanese Migrants by Continent of Destination

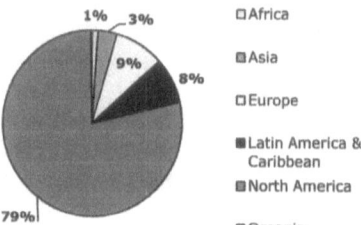

Notes: Values are not displayed if they are less than 1 percent.
Source: Human Development Report, 2009

Remittances Costs to Guyana from

	USA
Average cost of sending US$200	$17.68
Company with lowest cost	Laparkan
Lowest cost	$10.96

Notes: Corridor averages are unweighted and include
money transfer operators, banks and others.
Refers to the first quarter of 2010.

Source: Remittances Prices, World Bank, 2010

BIBLIOGRAPHY

Bernard, Keith (2007) *Remittance and the Dependency Syndrome* in HeartBeat News. P1-3

Best, Tony (2012). *Remittances to the Caribbean may Surge* in Carib News September 21, 2010 p.1

Betel, Paulette (2008) '*Caribbean Migration, Brain Drain and Remittances*', in Maxims News Network November, 6 2008.

Christie, Greg (2012) *Overcoming the problem of corruption in Jamaica.* Commentry-Jamaica Gleaner p2 September 21.

Hintzen, Percy (2001). West Indian immigrants : Self-Representation in an Immigrant Community, NY University Press.

Lall, G.H.K. Guyana (2012) : *A National Cesspool of Greed, Duplicity and Corruption*: A Re-migrant Story, September 1. Kindle.

McCabe, Kristen Caribbean (2011) *Migrants in the United States* in Migration Policy Institute April 7 p1-16.

Model, Suzanne (2008) *West Indian Immigrants: A Black Success Story* in Journal 'Society' November/December Issue.

Okonjo-Iweala, Ngozi. (2011) 12th William Demas Memorial Lecture (CDB) in Port of Spain' May 27.

Saunders, Sir Donald (2012) *A dark time for the Caribbean.* In Kaieteur News September 19. P1 features.

Reid, Ruel (2012); *Why we Must change the Caribbean Educational System* In BCNN October 5 p.1-2.

Persaud, Felicia, (2008). *The New Emerging US Niche Market* in Caribbean World News February 22.

Roberts, Michael (2007), *Systemic Caribbean Dependency,* in OPEd News p1-5

Part 11

—*Cultural Imperialism and the Caribbean* Part 111

Thomas, Kevin J, (2011). *Familial Influences on Poverty among children in Black Immigrant, US-Born Black, and non-Black Immigrant families.* Demography 48 (2): 437-460.

—(2012) *A Demographic Profile of Black Caribbean immigrants in the United States In Migration Policy Institute*

Ward Curtis A.: (2008) *Financial Crisis: Dilemma or Opportunity for Caribbean Diaspora. October.*

Index

A

acquired skills, 42
age groups, 15-16, 27-28
Americans, 23, 35, 44
Anguilla, 16-17
arrivals, piece, 45
Aruba, 17-18
assimilation, 22-23

B

Barbados, 9, 11, 13-14, 16-17, 22, 28, 31, 36, 45t
barrel, 22-23, 33-35, 47
Beckford, George, 8
Bernard, 40, 47, 81
Brazil road project, 8
Brooklyn, 14, 16
Burnham, Forbes, 8, 34, 47
businesses
    arcade-type, 17
    franchise food, 24
    passenger transportation, 46
    real estate, 19

C

Canada, 13, 19, 33, 36-37, 43
Caribbean
    governments, 10, 20, 23, 39, 42, 54
    immigrants, 13-14, 35
    nationals, 21, 23, 27, 35, 39
    region, 15, 33, 41
    residents, 15-18, 25-27
Caribbean, countries, 7-9, 12-13, 17, 31, 38-39, 46, 48-50
Caribbean, English-speaking, 14-15, 17-18, 21
CARICOM (Caribbean Community), 10, 12, 35, 49
Cayman Islands, 18
census, 14-15, 18, 43
Central America, 44
consumption patterns, 24, 26, 48
CSEC (Caribbean secondary education certificate), 15
Cuba, 13-14, 18
cultural imperialism, 35-36, 82
CXC (Caribbean Exams Council), 15, 28, 31

D

dependence, 8, 31, 35
developing countries, 11, 38
development, 8, 10, 21, 30, 34, 41,
    46-47, 53-54
diaspora, 23, 36, 39, 42, 46-48, 54, 82
dominant cultures, 31, 49-50
Dominican Republic, 13-14, 17, 19

E

earnings, 17-18
economic
  advancement, 36
  development, 38
  independence, 9, 23, 49
  issues, 22
education, 17, 19, 21, 23, 29, 31, 40, 46,
    49
employment, 9, 16-17, 19, 34-35, 39, 47
English, 13

F

fast-food mentality, 24
food, 15, 19, 23-25, 35
foreign countries, 19, 32-33, 35

G

Global Review Index of Caribbean
    Economic Freedoms, 10
Grenada, 9, 13, 16, 42, 45
growth, 8-10, 34, 40, 49, 53
Guadeloupe, 17, 19
Guyana, 8-9, 11, 13-14, 16-17, 22-23,
    28-29, 31, 33, 36-37, 39-40, 42-45,
    50, 81

H

Haiti, 13-14, 17, 42, 45
Hintzen, 41-42, 81

I

immigrants, 13-14, 16, 38, 50
industrial countries, 15, 31
industries
  labor-intensive, 8
  local shirt, 34
integration, 12, 19, 50, 53-54
Inter-American Development Bank, 37
Inter-American Dialogue, 38
interviews, 22, 24, 26, 43-44
investments, 8-9, 38

J

Jamaica, 8-9, 11, 13-14, 16-17, 19, 22,
    28, 30-31, 39, 42-43, 45, 50, 81
Jamaicans, 15, 28, 39, 41, 44
jobs, 17-19, 36, 39, 47, 53

K

knowledge, 25-28, 32, 49

L

Latin America, 37-38
LEP (limited English proficiency), 13
Lewis, David, 10

M

macroeconomic policies, 11
media, 23, 29, 44
migrants, 15, 17, 20, 24, 39, 42, 44-45,
    49-51, 81

migration, 22, 38, 41, 43, 45, 47, 50-51, 54, 81
money, 36-39, 44
money transfers. *See* remittances

N

National Development Strategy, 29
Netherlands Antilles, 17-18
North America, 30-31
nurses, 30-31, 43-44

O

outsourcing, 41

P

political
 dependency, 34
 independence, 7-9, 13, 19
poverty, 12, 35-36, 38, 40
products, 8-10, 34
professionals, 43-44
projects, 8, 11, 39, 42

R

Ravallion, Martin, 9
recruiters, 23, 30, 43-44
recruitment, 31, 43-44
remittances, 9, 15-18, 33, 35-39, 46-48, 50, 54, 81

resources, 12, 17, 41, 47-48
Returning Residents Program, 50
return migration, 50
Roberts, Michael, 12, 35, 49

S

salary, 44, 50
Saunders, Ronald, 10, 82
scholars, 8, 10, 12, 34, 43, 49, 54
skills, 8, 15, 19, 26, 30-32, 41, 43-44, 50-51, 53-54
SSEE (secondary schools entrance examination), 15

T

teachers, 23, 30-31, 43
television programs, 20, 23
tertiary-educated people, 30
Tobago, 9, 11, 13-14, 22, 30, 42, 44-45
trade, 9-10, 33-34
transfer, 39, 44, 46. *See also* remittances
Trinidad, 9, 11, 13-14, 16-17, 22, 28, 30-31, 39, 42, 44-45

U

United Kingdom, 13, 43-44
United States, 13-15, 17, 19, 21-24, 26, 29-30, 33-37, 40-41, 43, 45
US Census, 14, 21

www.ingramcontent.com/pod-product-compliance
Lightning Source LLC
Chambersburg PA
CBHW022126170526
45157CB00004B/1767